Edited by Eltin G

The Funeral Book

the columba press

First published, 1998, by
the columba press
55A Spruce Avenue, Stillorgan Industrial Park,
Blackrock, Co Dublin

Cover by Bill Bolger
Origination by The Columba Press
Printed in Ireland by Colour Books Ltd, Dublin

ISBN 1 85607 234 7

Contents

Preface   5

PART ONE

Making the Most of the Order of Christian Funerals
   Thomas R. Whelan CSSp   8

Funerals and Evangelisation
   Eltin Griffin O. Carm.   27

Parish Practicalities
   Desmond Forristal   31

November: Uniting memory and imagination in hope
   Dermot A. Lane   34

PART TWO: SAMPLE HOMILIES

Death of an older person   42

Death of a young person   58

Death of a child   85

Death of a parent   87

Death of a spouse   98

Death of a single person   101

Death of a pastor   103

Tragic death   107

Death after a long illness   118

Death of an autistic youth   123

Death of an unbeliever   125

The Contributors   128

Preface

Quite a slice of my life as a priest has gone into funeral ministry, from the old days when the ritual was virtually all in Latin, except for the prayers and gospel reading at the graveside, to the now more fully developed rites in the vernacular.

One has witnessed enormous change for the better. The specimen homilies in this book are in response to repeated requests. One hopes that would-be homilists will take advantage of the larger scenario provided here, the lengthy commentary on the funeral rites, the possibilities for evangelisation both in preaching and in the conduct of the ritual itself, sensitivity in the choice of readings for the funerals of particular individuals, and the topic of the month of November, with its fresh and exciting approach to eschatology.

We bring more than the externals of the rite to funeral celebrations. We bring ourselves, together with our assimilation of the Word of God and of the underlying theology of the rite. We bring sensitivity, a sense of prayer and compassion. Even though we are celebrating death, paradoxically, we can bring faith alive.

Eltin Griffin O. Carm.

PART ONE

Making the Most of
the Order of Christian Funerals

Thomas R. Whelan

Why Funeral Rites?

Death is an everyday occurrence and yet something inside us refuses to acknowledge it as 'normal'. When a relative or friend dies, we experience much more than grief due to a mere physical separation. The very question of *our own* mortality raises its head, and we find this difficult to deal with as it presents issues that touch us at the very core of our existence. Yet, we know that everyone who is born must die. There is a helplessness associated with death and dying, and we can only deal with this properly in the context of a wider horizon of meaning if we are to be rescued from despair. The rituals we employ at the time of the death and burial of a loved one serve to help us come to terms with a painful loss. They also attempt to offer meaning when all else seems to have failed.

Funerals: Rituals Surrounding Death

Funeral rites represent one of the most ancient and universal cultural forms in existence today. The rites that accompany and follow death serve a number of purposes which seem to go beyond any particular culture. They address basic human requirements in times of bereavement. Rituals surrounding death
- respond to a desire to pray for and accompany the deceased to his or her final resting place;
- create an 'environment' whereby those who mourn can be taken care of – in particular, through the offer of consolation and the reassurance of others;

8

– propose a context of hope, and a gentle but firm support. Mourners, and the wider community to which the deceased belonged, need to readjust their lives. Life from now on will be without their loved one.

Funeral rites, in any culture or belief system, are about much more than simple burial services. They help mark the stages of a painful journey and lead the bereaved to a new chapter in their lives.

Deeper reflection leads us to the realisation that the rites used must be capable of bearing the weight of the mystery of death. For a Christian, this mystery carries the added dimension of being understood in the context of Christ's death and resurrection. We quickly think also of the deceased's participation in the Easter mystery of Christ through baptism (see Rom 6:3-5). Furthermore, whatever rites used must be capable of helping mourners address their own fragility in the face of death and the question of the 'hereafter' which it raises, as well as their sense of loss and eventual readjustment.

Funerals: Journey with the Bereaved

It may be helpful for a moment to consider funeral rites as representing a type of 'rite of passage' – even if we do not wish to take the idea too far. 'Rites of Passage' refer to a journey that takes place in stages, beginning with a moment of 'separation', then moving through an 'in-between' or 'transition' stage, before arriving at a new 'coming together'. The *Order of Christian Funerals*[1] is made up of a complexity of rites, and in these some 'stages' may be operating at different levels at the same time.

There are many different moments and levels at which 'separation' occurs. For some people it can first present itself with the realisation that a relative or friend is dying. Another moment of separation happens at the time of death itself (or receiving news of the death). Levels of a realisation of 'finality' and separation emerge at other points, such as the gathering time with family (when the body has been prepared), or the more decisive closing of the coffin and, later, with burial itself. These different stages of leave-taking need to be suitably marked, if mourners are to eventually readjust themselves to life without their beloved one. There needs to be a 'closure' before people can move on.[2] Christian funeral practice does this with appropriate prayers and rites.

Funeral rites also serve to lead mourners gently through the 'in-between stage' while they are coming to terms with the death of their loved one. This transition stage knows no rules. The normal no longer applies. In fact, the 'normal' ceased with the news of the death of a loved one, and will only return – in a new way – when the bereaved come to terms with the trauma which has beset them. It is easy to understand the significance of ritual here. Family and friends may be dealing with many issues brought on by a death. Apart from those already mentioned (the question of mortality, and readjusting to a new situation), other matters sometimes arise. Faith concerns can emerge, maybe tinged with guilt and anger, not least for those for whom the Christian churches bear little relevance. Death throws family members into a new network of relationships that can either re-open wounds or bring with it an opportunity for healing. What was 'normal' is now open to question. One of the problems of our time is that modern culture attempts to telescope what used to take some time, into a few brief days. Society no longer offers the type of bereavement support it once did. In this respect, Christian funerals are, and ought to be, counter-cultural. They offer a framework within which gentle support and healing may be found. They play a central part in proposing faith to mourners as a helpful context for dealing with their new reality.

Respecting Ritual and Ritual Moments
The fluid and unsettling nature of this time demands that we

give due regard to the rituals that accompany death and burial. Often people have nothing else to hold onto apart from these rites.[3] This is certainly not a time to meddle with them, but rather to show profound respect for the rites themselves and the way they function. One of the many roles of ritual is to offer protection. It can provide a space that is defined by the comfort and security of the 'familiar', and within which one can feel safe and slowly regain a sense of 'normalcy'. Ritual, almost by definition, involves repetition, and this means employing prayers and gestures which are familiar through regular use. Working with the familiar is central to ritual activity – and never more so than during this 'transitional' time surrounding the death of a loved one. This point cannot be overemphasised.

Before looking at the *Order of Christian Funerals,* it might be helpful to make a few brief comments on the nature of ritual and its requirements.

* Good ritual places importance on the symbolic. Symbols should be full, generous, simple – and *unexplained.*
* Good ritual involves movement and gesture. Nothing can substitute for the security and comfort of a gentle hug or firm hand shake. Accompanying the body to the church and graveside is a gesture of solidarity and support.
* Gesture, like symbol, will reflect abundance and graciousness, largesse and warmth – without ever being patronising.
* A well-celebrated liturgy addresses reality through rites and symbols. This has the effect of locating our reality firmly in the context of a greater reality.
* Good ritual places much stock on fullness and on noble simplicity, on authenticity and on a sense of the mystery that these rites must bear.

Symbol and gesture are stronger than word. Certain experiences and moments in life are so traumatic that they are best expressed and responded to through symbol and gesture. When understood, the rites can be celebrated well and fully, and the *liturgy itself* can assume a ministerial role.

Good ritual behaviour means that those who lead liturgical prayer must themselves be familiar with the rites. A Presider would do well to page through the OCF, see how the various liturgies are structured, and how each rite relates to the overall. A Presider should also be familiar with the rich *resources* provided in the book. It is helpful to see what each element of the rite (be it gesture, a symbol, or a prayer text) communicates of our Christian belief at this time. A good starting place is the 'General Introduction' that prefaces the OCF. It is a relatively short but excellent text. It reflects an enormous degree of pastoral sensitivity and wisdom, gathered over a considerable period of time, from many countries throughout the world. The Irish edition benefits from this, and makes small modifications which reflect our pastoral and cultural practice. One should note the large selection of alternative ('Additional') texts on offer at the back of the book.

Order of Christian Funerals: Embodying our Faith

The OCF is the resource book of the parish community for its funerals. This book supplies a repertoire of rites, prayers and readings. It proposes an underlying structure that experience has shown to be most beneficial and supportive for the bereaved. It indicates how a faith climate might be created and sustained – one which would enable the bereaved mourn fully and regain a sense of equilibrium and meaning. A wise use of the OCF means that ministers will be able to approach funerals with resources appropriate to the pastoral circumstances which present themselves. A knowledge of the 'General Introduction', and the introductions which preface each section of the book, will help a pastoral ministry to be creative in how to communicate to the bereaved a faith-filled understanding of death and journeying. Let us briefly highlight something of the vision which this liturgical ritual reveals.

The first observation to be made is that funeral rites are about more than just burial procedures. They form part of a large pastoral ministry to the sick, the dying and the bereaved. A local assembly should be prepared to accompany those of its members who are seriously sick. They will do this through their prayer as well as through those who, in various ways, perform a ministry to the sick. Pastoral care will often continue long after the burial so that the bereaved can be accompanied through the 'transitional' period until they come to terms with their new situation. The practice of a 'month's mind' and anniversary Mass – common in some places – contribute to this process of re-integration.

A second point to note is the vision of 'church' found in the OCF. Ministry to the dying and the bereaved is not the preserve of the priest. The *full community* has responsibility to offer a faith-filled support. This can take many forms. Obviously a community which has a consciousness of its all-year-round immersion into the mystery of Christ's death and resurrection, will be well equipped to offer a faith context for those who are mourning. Specifically, bereavement groups form an important part of an overall ministry. The local assembly should be there to sustain and, often, simply to 'be with' family and close friends, when a loved one is dying or has died.

Baptism supplies the OCF with metaphors and a language with which to speak of death. Reading through the prayers and scripture texts, one cannot but be struck by the many references and allusions to baptism. We begin our Christian lives with baptism. Paul described baptism as a death. When initiated, we are plunged into the death of Christ so that we might experience now – if only imperfectly and imperceptibly – resurrection-life in Christ. At our own death, we are brought fully into its completion in Christ.

Another image we meet is that of 'eternal life'. Again the roots of this are to be found in the initiation sacraments. Baptism immersed us in God's trinitarian life. This is something we are destined to continue when we are called to fullness of life at death, but in a way far greater than anything we could ever perceive. Ministers are encouraged by the OCF to proclaim the victory of life over death.

Walking through the Order of Christian Funerals

Funeral rites are principally concerned with the final journey that a community makes with its deceased loved one. A task must be accomplished. The dead must be buried. Christian liturgy places a person's death, and the sorrow of the mourners, in the context of Christ's death and our baptismal immersion into that death. We pray for the deceased and allow our faith in the resurrection to sustain those who are bereaved.

The principal ritual unfolds in three moments. *Receiving the body at the church* is customary in Ireland on the evening before the burial. The central funeral liturgy (which normally includes a celebration of the Eucharist) incorporates the *Rite of Commendation and Farewell.* The procession of journey follows, accompanying the coffin to the place of committal.

I. RECEPTION OF THE BODY AT THE CHURCH

After the initial (biblical) greeting of those present, the coffin is sprinkled with blessed water. Where the baptismal fountain is near the door, this might take place as the coffin is brought past, using water from the fountain itself (even if this means taking water from the font into the bucket). In this way the opening words of the prayer, 'In the waters of baptism ...', (and subsequent references to baptism) become highlighted by the ritual gesture.

A Note on Blessed Water. The ritual suggests, for certain occasions, the use of blessed water: on the occasion of gathering in the presence of the body; at the conclusion of a vigil; at the time of the closing of the coffin, where it is described as 'a gesture' (III) and at the time of committal. The sprinkling is presumed at the reception in the church, and during the final commendation. The OCF (36) notes that the use of blessed water primarily evokes a reminder of the deceased's 'initiation into the community of faith'. The obvious links with baptism can be enhanced when the sprinkling is carried out in an un-rushed and generous way, using a traditional sprinkler or an evergreen branch. If circumstances permit, there is no reason why the Presider would not place his hand in the font and sprinkle the coffin in a gracious and dignified manner.

A pall, 'a sign of the Christian dignity of the person' (38), may now be placed on the coffin by family members, friends or the minister (139). It is done in silence.

A Note on the Pall: Communities for whom the use of the Pall is not customary could do well to consider introducing it. It is a large white cloth, of simple design, capable of covering the coffin, and made of good quality cloth. It recalls the baptismal garment put on by the newly baptised, and therefore speaks of quiet and confident hope. As it is a symbol, there should be no designs, texts or other symbols superimposed on it. It covers the coffin during the liturgy, and serves to signify 'that all are equal in the eyes of God' (Jas 2:1-9), (38).[4]

The Presider leads the way to the central part of the church. An appropriate song is sung during this procession, unless 'serious pastoral difficulties prevent this' (123). The rite suggests a number of possibilities (140). If the assembly is not yet accustomed to a fuller music ministry, then a song leader or cantor could lead with some suitable music. A simple antiphon or refrain sung by all to a spoken text is often very effective, and is easy to do.

The ministry of music at funerals
(a) Why music? 'Music is integral to the funeral rites. It allows the community to express convictions and feelings that words

alone may fail to convey. It has the power to console and uplift the mourners and to strengthen the unity of the assembly in faith and love' (30). Its importance cannot be underestimated.

(b) Its Function? Whatever music is used, it should 'support, console, and uplift the participants and should help to create in them a spirit of hope in Christ's victory over death and in the Christian's share in that victory' (31). The texts 'should express the paschal mystery of the Lord's suffering, death, and triumph over death and should be related to the readings from scripture' (30).[5]

(c) The choice of music is not guided by a list of the deceased's favourites. Music and text should bear some relation to the mystery of Christ being celebrated.

(d) The practice of 'hiring' or importing a soloist for the occasion goes against good taste, and has missed the point about how music functions in relation to the liturgical assembly. An increasing number of communities are developing a music ministry to serve their funeral needs. Parishes can develop a specific ministry of funeral cantor or musician.

The Easter candle will have been placed beforehand near where the coffin will rest. A family member, friend, or the Presider may now place a symbol of Christian life on the coffin. The OCF supplies possible short texts to accompany this gesture. However, if done gracefully and without haste, with no other action taking place, this can be carried out quite effectively in silence.

A Note on the Christian Symbols:
(a) *A Book of Gospels:* A Bible (maybe even that of the deceased) may be carried in procession from the door, and placed on the coffin at this time. This gesture underlines the importance of the Word of God in the living of Christian life. It also draws attention to the call to be faithful to that Word if we wish to be part of God's kingdom (38).

(b) Alternatively, a cross may be placed on top of the coffin. This symbol highlights the faith statement that we have been called to live our lives by the cross with which we have been marked in baptism. It proclaims the great Christian enigma, that the cross is the way to resurrection and life.

It is good to note OCF 38: 'Only Christian symbols may rest on or be placed near the coffin during the funeral liturgy. Any other symbols, for example, national flags, or flags or insignia of associations, have no place in the funeral liturgy' (see also 120). Symbols refer to that which speaks of Christian hope and the person's baptismal life and immersion into Christ's death and resurrection. Personal items associated with the deceased's past life are best used at services apart from the funeral rites. *Mass Cards* can be collected in a basket placed in some convenient location. *Wreaths* can be arranged somewhere to the side, from where they will be later brought to the place of burial. When either appear on or beside the coffin, they tend to distract from the simplicity, beauty and directness of the Christian symbols used.

The Opening Prayer follows. Presiders should be aware of the very large selection of prayers for different circumstances found in the appendix. The ritual notes that the reading of the Word of God, which follows, 'is the high point and central focus of the reception rite' (124). Unless it is impossible to do so, the responsorial psalm should be sung. At the very least, the response itself could be sung by all, with the verses read.

A sense of pastoral responsibility will guide in the choice of appropriate readings. Their purpose is to proclaim the paschal mystery, and to offer gentle and hope-filled support to the assembly in its bereavement. The readings present a context for understanding what is happening: a vision of God's kingdom presented by Jesus. The ritual notes that the 'brief homily' which follows is based on the readings, and 'is not a eulogy' (145). A litany of intercession leads to a suitable Concluding Prayer and Concluding Rite.

This liturgy marks an important moment in the journey of farewell to a loved one. Before burial, the community receive the body of the deceased in their place of worship. This is the place where people enter into a new life. They are immersed by baptism into the mystery of Christ's saving death. Here the assembly is nourished in the eucharist, as was the deceased. The various baptismal symbols, gestures and images of this liturgy gives expression to a reverence we wish to show towards the body, a temple of God's presence. They also create the context that will inspire the community's funeral prayers as it buries one of its own: a hope informed by faith. Thus enabled, the community offers consolation and support to the family and friends of the deceased. It marks a stage in the process of separation. Normally the rite of reception is not celebrated with Mass, unless this is to be the funeral Mass.[6]

2. FUNERAL MASS
FINAL COMMENDATION AND FAREWELL

'The funeral Mass is the central liturgical celebration of the Christian community for the deceased' (150).

It is appropriate that the community should gather just one more time in the presence of the deceased, and do what they do together each Sunday – keep the memory of the Lord as they celebrate eucharist.[7] The eucharist says all that we want to say about the life-giving death of Christ, into which mystery we were initiated through baptism. It also enables us interpret the death of a deceased person against the death of Christ. It offers us a foretaste of the heavenly banquet to which all are invited. Eucharistic communion unites all the faithful, living and dead, with Christ.

The OCF offers a fine commentary on the funeral Mass (153-

162), which goes into considerable detail when discussing certain of its elements. There is an obvious desire that this central funeral liturgy would sustain the bereaved at this time of sorrow, and that the mystery of Christ would give reason for their hope. It notes especially that the entrance procession should be accompanied by the singing of a suitable song. What was said above regarding music applies here also. Songs should reflect 'profound expression of belief in eternal life and the resurrection' as well as interceding for the deceased (153). Likewise, the OCF presumes that the responsorial psalm is sung, using one of the many ways in which this can be done. There is no shortage of suitable music resources available. Simple acclamations are easily used during other parts of the liturgy, especially during the eucharistic prayer and communion rite.

Members of the family of the deceased, or friends, may bring to the altar the gifts to be used in the eucharist. The purpose of this short rite ('Presentation of the Gifts') is simply so that the next part of the liturgy can take place. It is not appropriate at this time to carry up 'symbols' of the life of the deceased or personal momentos. To add 'symbols' at this stage is to attempt to make the ritual say something different. A suitable occasion for using personal momentos might well be during a vigil, before or after the reception of the body, or during a brief remembrance of the deceased at the final commendation and farewell.

At the end of the liturgy, the community make their final farewell to one of their own whom they now entrust to the loving mercy of God. The tone changes. We now hear the language of 'separation' and of hope. We recall the invitation extended through Christ, that we enter into his heavenly kingdom. Voice is given in the prayers to our faith, which tells us that we will be reunited, one day, with our deceased sisters and brothers.[8]

This beautiful rite takes place after the prayer after communion (the blessing and dismissal are omitted). It should not be overloaded. It marks the beginning of the final stage of 'separation' which concludes with burial. The change in emotional intensity at this point is best responded to by *ritual simplicity*. Extra commentary, explanations or prayers should not be added to what is already offered. Important, for instance, is the period of silent prayer (181) which takes place after the opening invitation to prayer. Silence is essential here to help in the transition to this final part of the liturgy.

Parish communities with even the most modest means should be able to sing some suitable song of farewell.[9] It is a high-point of this rite. This song (along with the prayer and gesture used here) gives expression to the great hope that we will one day be able to join with our deceased sisters and brothers and, with one voice, sing the praises and glory of God. It is a song which gives utterance to a companionship and a communion between heaven and earth, to a sense of urgency in wanting to be in the presence of the Almighty, to a feeling of 'going home'. If we examine the texts and rite, we see that the final commendation is all about commending the deceased to God, and bidding farewell in prayer and song.

The abundant sprinkling of the coffin with blessed water and profuse incensing – all calmly done – may take place before, during, or after the song of farewell. These gestures give expression to the dignity with which the community upholds the body of the deceased. This person, through baptism, became a living temple of God's presence, and these are signs of farewell. Incense is 'a sign of the community's prayers for the deceased rising to the throne of God' (37). Sufficient incense should be used so that its meaning is self-evident. The prayer of commendation concludes the rite. The final part of the journey to the resting place now begins, and a suitable song or psalm should accompany the procession with the coffin.

3. RITE OF COMMITTAL

The Rite of Committal is simple and direct: short scripture read-ing, prayer over the place of burial, committal, intercessions, and finally, concluding prayer over the people. The rite allows for the sprinkling of the grave and coffin with blessed water and the use of incense, if this is customary. This is practical when a burial takes place at a graveside near to the church. When the place of committal is some distance from the church, a sense of dignity and simplicity suggests that incense and blessed water are not used, unless this can be easily done. The practice of using small plastic bottles of blessed water, hastily sprinkled over coffin and grave, does nothing to express the mystery of baptism, or a respectful Christian farewell.

The custom of scattering some earth on the coffin, where used, ought to be encouraged. It forms an important part of the leave-taking which is being expressed here in a very decisive manner. By making a 'closure' here, the road towards healing and the later stages of bereavement is facilitated. It also helps to give ritual poignancy to the prayers which, at this moment and later, express with deep faith, hope in resurrection.

4. RELATED RITES

Among other funeral rites offered by the OCF are:

Prayers after Death – which may be suitably used when the minis-ter makes an initial contact with the family after the death has occurred;

Gathering in the Presence of the Body – a resource which may be found helpful for 'when the family first gathers in the presence of the body, when the body is to be prepared for burial, or after it has been prepared' (60).

Vigil for the Deceased – described as the 'principal rite celebrated by the Christian community' between the death and the funeral liturgy. It is ideal, also, for when a wake takes place;

Transfer of the Body to the Church – to be celebrated normally before the closing of the coffin, as family and friends prepare to bring the body of the deceased to the church.

Each rite is preceded by a very short, but excellent, pastoral commentary. Provision is also made for situations in which lay people will preside and lead the prayer.

Familiarity with these is helpful if they are to be used appropriately and sensitively. The options available should be noted, as well as the rich collections of additional texts found at the back of the ritual book. Each rite, in its own way, marks another stage in the journey. They all belong to an 'in-between' stage between receiving the news of the death, the burial, and taking up, once again, normal living. They address situations in which the bereaved must deal with a variety of emotions which may include sorrow, confusion, anger, and emptiness. Prayer leaders should also bear in mind that the mourners present may range from those who are faith-filled believers to those for whom the church bears little relevance. These liturgies ritualise simple gestures (such as the sealing of the coffin and beginning the journey to the church) or necessary happenings (such as making contact with the family immediately after death has taken place, or at the time when the body is prepared for burial). Ritual, in its simplicity and directness, helps articulate the grief and sorrow of those close to the deceased, and quietly offers them the support of the wider church community. The short prayers and verses of scripture gently remind them of a God who is with them in their pain and confusion. These rites are best celebrated without commentary, explanation, or addition. They are short, but should never be rushed. Their simplicity and directness are best respected.

Other rites are supplied to address occasions when the customary pattern is not followed. There is a rite for the *Reception of the Body before the Funeral Mass,* used when the funeral liturgy is to take place immediately. The *Funeral Liturgy outside Mass* is available for use on those days when a funeral Mass is not possible (Holy Thursday, Easter Triduum, Sundays of Advent, Lent and Easter), and when pastoral or other circumstances suggest this to be the best option. Part II of the ritual presents *Funeral Rites for Children*. An appendix gives the *Rite of Committal at a Crematorium*.

A few words about the Vigil of Prayer. It follows the normal liturgical format: introductory rites, liturgy of the word, intercessions, and concluding rite (see 69-98). The Vigil can be used in the presence of the body, at home or in a funeral parlour, and is very suitable during a wake. It is to be regretted that the Irish edition does not offer the possibility of celebrating a part of the liturgy of the hours here (or at the reception of the body at the church). This is a realistic possibility for religious communities and for any other group used to or comfortable with this ancient liturgical prayer. A simple 'cathedral' form of this prayer is possible.

The wake is no longer a normal feature of Irish burial custom. When it takes place, it plays an important social and ritual function, not simply in offering support to a family in the immediate aftermath of a death, but also in the 'remembering' that takes place at such a gathering. The need to remember and recount the story of the deceased is deep, and needs 'ritual space' for it to happen. When it cannot take place here (where it is probably more appropriate), it needs to take place later. However, it should never displace the homily at a funeral Mass.

5. LITURGICAL MINISTRY

A useful context for understanding how liturgical ministry is best exercised is indicated by the realisation that it is the church which gathers to mourn the death of one of its own. It is therefore the church community which supplies ministers on such occasions. Given the fact that most funerals take place on weekdays, some parishes have a group of ministers who offer their services for funerals, so that the liturgy might be celebrated with the care it deserves. Appropriate liturgical ministries include those common in any parish: readers, musicians, hospitality, and special ministers of the eucharist, as well as pall bearers.

If ministers of hospitality are available, they can contribute greatly to putting mourners at ease as they arrive, especially those who may not be familiar with Catholic practices, or who are not regular church-goers. Consideration needs to be given to the ministry of reader. Should family members be the principal or even sole source for liturgical ministry? A balance needs to be kept between enabling members to participate in this ministry, and having readings badly proclaimed by people who are not accustomed to reading in liturgy, or who may find themselves unable to read properly due to their grief. Other opportunities for encouraging family members and friends of the deceased to participate actively, include the placing of the pall on the coffin at the reception of remains, the placing of Christian symbols on the coffin (if this is being done), and leading the prayers of intercession. They should be encouraged to take as active a part as circumstances and their grief allow. It is interesting that with regard to musicians, the OCF 170 considers a cantor and an organist (or other instrumentalists) as normative. They serve to assist the assembly in singing the relevant parts. A choir is considered optional.

Conclusion

The *Order of Christian Funerals* is the resource book for the Christian rites which surround the death of a believer. Careful use of and selection from a repertoire of rites and Christian symbols assist those who mourn to readjust themselves to the human loss they experience. It helps support them in their pain by its calm and faith-filled assurance of the resurrection of Christ, and all that this means. The Easter mystery of Christ transforms, and offers, not just hope, but a context for understanding all death. The OCF concerns itself principally with the central ritual moments which lead the family and assembly on the journey of farewell from home or hospital, to church, and to grave. A wider bereavement ministry will assist the mourners on their continuing journey. Local custom will suggest the importance to be attached to the Month's Mind and First Anniversary Mass, which also form part of the community's ministry to the bereaved as they go through their final stages of readjustment.

The funeral rites will at all times gently and comfortingly allow Christian hope and faith inform the way it supports and journeys with its mourners, that they may come to terms with the reality which has invaded their lives. When circumstances permit, the family and friends of a deceased person can grow into a deep awareness and appreciation of how the paschal mystery of Christ, into which we were all immersed through baptism, can enrich our understanding of God's plan.

Notes

1. *Order of Christian Funerals* (Dublin: Veritas Publications, 1991) (hereafter OCF). Paragraph numbers will be referred to without any prefix.

2. Placing a board with artificial grass over the grave rather than throwing earth on the coffin (as is the custom in some local places), can delay or deny a final separation. One could well ask, to what extent does this make both the social and psychological transition to the next stage of bereavement more difficult?

3. It is important to acknowledge the meaning that ritual can have at moments like this, even to those who rarely, if ever, go to church.

4. 'For this reason, any national flag or the flags or insignia of associations to which the deceased belonged are to be *removed* from the coffin at the entrance of the church. They may be replaced after the coffin has been taken from the church' (120). Dennis C. Smolarski notes that 'The ritual adds the words "even Christian associations" and even includes the phrase

"or symbols of ministry". These specifications in the Canadian edition try to emphasise that those things that distinguish people during life – military service, membership in Catholic fraternal organisations, even ordained ministers within the church – must not distinguish the dead, who are equal before God.' (*Sacred Mysteries: Sacramental Principles and Liturgical Practice,* New York/ Mahwah, NJ: Paulist Press, 1995:145).

5. There is much simple and easily accessible music readily available. The following could be mentioned: the music cards, published by Veritas Publications, Dublin, *Music for Funerals* (1994), and *Music for Removal of Remains* (1998); and the collection edited by Stephen Dean, *Music for the Funeral Rite* (Great Wakering, Essex: McCrimmons, 1991). The OCF itself offers a few excellent melodic settings – and, in doing so, points to what ought, as a minimum, to be sung.

6. When the reception of the body takes place before the funeral Mass, the relevant section of the OCF is followed. The rite follows the same pattern as outlined above up to the placing of Christian symbols on the coffin. The Presider then makes the customary reverence of the altar, using incense if appropriate, and then beginning the Opening Prayer of Mass. It should be noted that the normal introductory rites of Mass are omitted: sign of cross, greeting, and penitential rite.

7. When the funeral Mass must take place on a Sunday, pastoral sensitivity will help choose between retaining all or some of the readings and prayers proper to the Sunday, or using those of the funeral liturgy. It is never appropriate to use funeral texts and readings on Sundays of Advent, Lent and Easter, or on solemnities of obligation. The readings on these occasions, however, provide a wonderful context for speaking about the death of a Christian.

8. The final commendation and farewell is always used, be it as a conclusion of the funeral Mass or other liturgy, or at the cemetery.

9. Other suitable texts are offered in the appendix, OCF 318.

Funerals and Evangelisation

Eltin Griffin O. Carm.

Preaching has to do with mystery. It has to do with the mystery of Christ as it applies to a particular celebration. The ultimate mystery for most people in our day is the mystery of death. In a world of such amazing and vast technological achievement, death is the great stumbling block. Thirty years ago, the Vatican II *Pastoral Constitution on the Church in the Modern World* gave voice to this concern in an oft quoted paragraph (18). 'It is in regard to death that our condition is most shrouded in doubt. We are tormented not only by pain and the gradual breaking up of the body but also, and even more, by the dread of ceasing to be. But a deep instinct leads us rightly to shrink from and to reject the utter ruin and total loss of the personality. Because we bear within ourselves the seed of eternity which cannot be reduced to mere matter, we rebel against death. All aids, made available by technology, however useful they may be, cannot set our anguished minds at rest. They may prolong one's lifespan; but this does not satisfy the heart-felt longing, one that can never be stifled, for a life to come.' (*Vatican Council II Documents*, ed. Flannery, 1975. Adapted, with permission, to eliminate sexist language.)

This is the background against which one preaches a homily at a funeral in our time. One views it, as it were, through the prism of Christ's own death and resurrection. One views it also through the prism of the Word of God chosen for the occasion. Funeral preaching provides a unique opportunity for evangelisation. Persons who seldom visit a church, or who declare quite openly that they have no religious affiliation, will put in an appearance at the funeral Mass or at the removal on the previous evening. Good preaching which brings the Word to life and relates it to this particular occasion can have quite an impact. Communication, though, occurs at many other levels apart from the spoken word. The very way the presider introduces the celebration, his gestures, the vestments and how he wears them, their colour, texture and design, the way he invites the readers and others concerned, can make for communication at the deeper level of feeling. An evident healthy respect between the priest, the other ministers and the gathered people, will speak louder than the words. So can the atmosphere that emanates from a church or a parish where a developed sense of community and participation is evident. It is not a case of preaching only, but of preaching allied to witness. Pope John Paul II exhorts: 'We need heralds of the gospel who are experts in humanity, who know the depths of the human heart, who can share the joys and the hopes, the agonies and distress of people today, who are at the same time contemplatives who have fallen in love with God. For this we need the saints of today.'

Funeral Homilies

Homilies at funeral Masses can be problematic in some parishes where funerals tend to be frequent. It is difficult to be fresh on every occasion especially if, as sometimes happens, the funeral takes place at a late morning Mass which has its regular quota of attenders who may not be directly concerned with the obsequies. Here, too, the particular has to be merged with the general. The Presider, in the Introduction to the *Order of Christian Funerals*, has been described as 'a teacher of the faith and the minister of consolation'. On him falls the burden of knitting the whole celebration together. One is celebrating the passing away, or more correctly, the passover, of a particular woman, man or, tragically, of a particular child.

The homily should never become a eulogy, but of course discreet allusion to the Christian witness of the deceased, or to the human qualities which endeared them to others, will not be out of place. Neither will a well-timed insertion of humour in regard to an older person, or a recall of personal characteristics, provided that the gist of the homily is centred on mystery. Not with the mystery of death itself, in the sense of why did one have to die. That can be sterile and can lead the hearers into an intellectual cul-de-sac. So can concern about life after death. Rather should the concern be with life through death, as happened with Christ, whose Paschal Mystery is the paradigm for a Christian's passing over to eternal life.

The Twist

What matters most in the special occasion homily is the particular twist that the preacher can give to his homily. A lot will depend upon the circumstances of the death and on the readings chosen for the occasion. Homilies given in tragic circumstances – suicide, accident, unexpected death or the death of a child – can have enormous power if the Word suits the occasion. One picks up a lot of detail in a very short space of time as one visits the home, talks with the family, with neighbours and with relatives. One twigs to a lot in what are usually very crowded hours for the family.

The Word

The Lectionary offers a fairly good choice of readings. I have sometimes opted for the gospel of the previous Sunday. Desmond Forristal, parish priest at Dalkey, Co Dublin, has a very lovely piece concerning the choice of readings in this volume.

A Larger Package

The homily, important though it may be, never stands on its own. It is part of a larger package. A friend of mine, a parish priest, travelled to some part of the United States to be with his brother in his illness and to celebrate the obsequies. He decided to check out the final details with the local church. He called the rectory only to be told that 'Father says you'll find it all in the book'. It is never all in the book. The book, admirable though it may be in many of its details, is more like the script of a play or the libretto of a musical to be rendered at the appropriate time and place. No two funeral services can ever be the same. One has always to adapt the rite to the occasion. One does not necessarily change anything, but the book as such offers a wide variety of options for prayers, prefaces, blessings and readings. Like good stories, it all depends on the way you tell them. It all depends, too, on the way you read or proclaim the various items, on the accompanying gestures, on the right pauses and emphases.

Music, for most people at a time of grief, can also make a big impact. Visiting musicians can wreck a service if they are not sensitive to the deeper spiritual meaning of the Funeral Rite and are able to choose music accordingly. One can only praise the efforts of parishes who try to provide an 'ad hoc' weekday choir for funerals, the successor surely of voluntary groups in the past who attended to the dead, or to what was known in Dublin as the 'Bona Mors' Confraternity.

 I have seldom found a Prayer of the Faithful to excel the formula on page 1003 of the Roman Missal for sheer richness of expression. It can be given as a model to the relatives to which they can add their own particular concerns.

Compassion
Compassion is the heart of all Christian ministry, and more particularly, at the heart of funeral ministry. With regard to the preaching, Henri J. M. Nouwen includes this little nugget somewhere: 'What is addressed to the few gains the attention of the many.'

Parish Practicalities

Desmond Forristal

The phone rings. Even before he identifies himself, I recognise the voice of one of our local undertakers. (I think they prefer to be called Funeral Directors these days, but to the plain people of Ireland they are and always will be undertakers.) Would Tuesday at 5.30 be all right for the removal of the remains? And the funeral after 10 o'clock Mass on Wednesday to Shanganagh cemetery? Yes, that would be all right.

Priests are being criticised these days for all kinds of reasons, and sometimes for no reason at all. But at a time of death and bereavement, the priest is accepted and indeed welcomed in homes which might otherwise be closed to him. Grief is grief the whole world over but it is made easier to bear when there is an ordered ritual to follow, not merely in the church and the grave-yard, but also in the home itself. The women making tea in the kitchen, the neighbours bringing round cakes and sandwiches, the concerned callers steaming up the garden path, are all means of coping with reality. 'I'm sorry for your trouble,' may not be the most eloquent of condolences but it is confirmed by custom and sealed by sincerity.

The visit of the priest
The visit of the priest is part of the process. He may have been there the day before to administer the last rites, but the visit after the death has a character of its own. He meets the members of the family, arriving jet-lagged from foreign parts. He listens, a sympathetic audience of one, to their reminiscences about the

departed. He discusses the funeral Mass, the hymns, the readings, the prayer of the faithful. He says a Hail Mary or a decade of the rosary before he departs, leaving the family busily discussing the relative merits of the Book of Wisdom and St Paul to the Romans, and wondering whether Uncle Joe should be asked to sing *Panis Angelicus* at the communion or not.

In our church, as in most churches, the funeral Mass is usually at 10 o'clock. There is a large regular congregation at that Mass, the majority of them tending towards the elderly. Often the deceased person has been a regular attender at the Mass. The 10 o'clock congregation is a kind of little community, where all the regulars know one another to see but rarely know one another's names. 'Who was she?' 'You knew her well, the little old lady in the blue coat who always knelt beside St Joseph's statue.' I heard of a church in America where they put up a photograph of the deceased on the notice board. It sounds like a good idea but somehow I don't think we're ready for it yet.

Liturgy of the Word

There is a good choice of readings for funeral Masses in the lectionary. But we are free to choose others. The gospel may be chosen to highlight some aspect of the dead person's life. For the little old lady in the blue coat who always knelt beside St Joseph's statue, one could use the description of Anna in the Temple, or the story of the widow who put her little contribution into the treasury. Simeon and his *Nunc Dimittis* would be suitable for an elderly man. The call of St Matthew for a business man. The calming of the storm at sea for a mariner. The parable of the sower for a farmer or gardener. The Good Samaritan for a social worker. Martha and Mary for a housewife. For a young person, the raising of the little girl or the widow's son at Naim. For a young child, Jesus and the children. The possibilities are endless.

The homily should have the same variety. And it should be brief. We have to remember the regular Mass-goers as well as the mourners. Nothing is more trying to them than the priest who gives the same interminable homily at every funeral Mass. It upsets their whole morning schedule, apart from the fact that they've heard it all before. A few well-chosen sentences about the deceased, a word of condolence to the family, and a message of Christian hope from the readings, should not take more than five minutes. While we naturally say only good things about the deceased (not always an easy task), we are not there to canonise them. We are not entitled to say that they are enjoying their reward. There is One who judges. We are there to pray for them.

Seventy-two candles

Once a year, on All Souls' Day, we think of all our dead. For several years we tried to think of some visual statement in our church that would sum up the meaning of the day. Nothing seemed to work. Various arrangements of crosses, candles, flowers, plants were tried in vain. One year we resurrected the traditional catafalque, a coffin-shaped board covered by a richly embroidered black drape. It was a disaster. Everyone wanted to know who was dead. Even when it was explained to them, they still hated it.

Then last year, we finally got it right. We borrowed two long plastic flower containers, draped them in purple, filled them with sand and gravel, and put them up on the reredos behind the altar, one on either side of the tabernacle. Into them we set seventy-two candles and lit them, one for each of the seventy-two people who had been buried from the church during the preceding twelve months. The evening Mass on All Souls' Day included a service of reconciliation after the gospel. The packed congregation, the dimmed lights (we have dimmers on all our lights), and the seventy-two candles flickering away in the sanctuary, spoke more powerfully than any human words. These are our dead and we have not forgotten them.

November:
Uniting memory and imagination in hope

Dermot A. Lane

We are living at a time in which there is a serious eclipse of hope affecting the quality of political and religious life. At worst, there is an ever increasing amount of cynicism concerning the political process and a growing apathy regarding religion. At best, there are traces of optimism in politics and religion. What is needed more than ever before is a strong, prophetic theology of hope that will disturb both church and society and transform their respective complacencies.

The month of November is a time when the Christian community remembers its dead. In particular, during November the church's liturgy celebrates the feast of All Saints, commemorates all the faithful departed, and previews in the Sunday readings the end of the world. The underlying assumption within the church's liturgy throughout November is the centrality of hope. Two of the most important elements within any theology of hope are memory and imagination. It is imagination that sparks off hope and memory that keeps hope alive. To be sure, there are other dimensions to hope such as trust, love, story, and a creation-centred faith. In this short reflection we will confine ourselves to some preliminary remarks on the role of memory and the place of imagination in the birth of hope, in view of their liturgical importance for the month of November.

The power of memory
Contemporary philosophy and theology have rehabilitated the importance of memory to a remarkable degree. Memory is an

important ingredient in the construction of human identity and the shaping of human consciousness. A balanced understanding of who we are arises out of our capacity to be connected through memory with the past. Memory enables the past to influence the present. To remember is to make alive what has been cut off from us through death.

The kind of memory we are talking about here is not that which simply recalls the good old days, nor is it merely the memory that indulges sentimentally in some past golden age. Instead it is the memory that is true to the past in a manner that has power to disrupt and interrupt the coziness of the present. It is the memory that has the capacity to interrupt the tyranny of the present. Above all, the memory in question is one that enables us to realise that the way we are is not the way we have to be; it is a memory that has the ability to activate a praxis that breaks through the prevailing historical consciousness as if it were an irreformable given.

To remember the dead as we do in November is to make alive again those who have been cut off from us. This process of remembering is about putting back together what has been dismembered from us. By remembering the dead we recover something of the fundamental unity and solidarity of the whole human family. This sense of unity between the living and the dead – which is symbolised through the Christian doctrine of the Communion of Saints and perhaps more fully by the commemoration of all the dead – is an important step in the genesis of hope. I cannot hope alone – but I can begin to hope in solidarity with the dead and the living.

It is instructive to note in passing how the dead have been remembered in the past through monuments like Newgrange in Ireland and the Pyramids in Egypt – powerful symbols of ancestral unity.

To disconnect ourselves from the past is to cut ourselves off from one of the important sources of human identity. We are what we are in virtue of our dead. Those who sever their solidarity with the dead, all too quickly end up severing their solidarity with the living. This, in turn, leads to hopeless forms of individualism symbolised in the self-sufficiency of modern self. In contrast, Gabriel Marcel points out: 'Hope is only possible on the level of us, or we might say *agape* ... it does not exist on the level of the solitary ego.' (G. Marcel, *Homo Viator: An Introduction to a Metaphysic of Hope,* London: V. Gollancz, 1951:10). A close correlation seems to exist between the rise of individualism and the eclipse of hope today.

Memory in the Judaeo-Christian tradition

It is no mere coincidence that memory plays a crucial role in the life of Judaism and Christianity. Judaism is about remembering the passover experience and God's covenant with the people of Israel. Likewise in Christianity it is the memory of the crucified and risen Christ, celebrated in the eucharist, that sustains the Christian community in hope. The memory of Jesus, his preaching about the reign of God, his open table-fellowship, his unconditional offer of forgiveness, and especially his saving death and resurrection, activates hope in the present and the future. This memory of Jesus is often described as a liberating, 'dangerous' and disturbing memory.

The most appropriate place, therefore, for the Christian to remember the dead is in the celebration of the eucharist. In the eucharist we remember the dead no longer as dead but as alive in Christ, no longer as past but as present to us in the Christian assembly. In the eucharist, through the memory of the passion, death and resurrection of Christ, our unity with the past is recovered, hope in the present is renewed, and the future is anticipated. When we celebrate the eucharist, the pastness of the dead and the deadness of the past are transformed into a new dynamic reality in the present that shapes our understanding of the future. It is this extraordinary power of memory, particularly effective in the eucharist, that generates hope. If it is true to say that memory is an important ingredient in the genesis of hope, then it is equally true to assert that it is imagination that sustains hope in existence.

The role of imagination

When imagination becomes dulled or deadened, or when the imagination finds itself caught in between paradigm shifts, which represents our present experience, then one of the first casualties is hope. A close connection exists between imagination and hope.

In talking about imagination, we need to get away from the popular misunderstanding that imagination is about the fanciful projection of an unreal world. To the contrary, imagination is about the human capacity to construct a coherent world of meaning out of the connections that exist between a variety of different images. Imagination is about knowing and understanding the world around us. In particular, imagination is about the capacity to construct new and alternative possibilities out of our experience of the world in which we live. It is this innate and irrepressible capacity to image life differently and alternatively that keeps hope in existence. It is important, therefore, to distinguish between the fanciful imagination and the realistic imagination.

The imagination that sustains hope in existence is not the private imagination of the isolated individual but the imagination that is in touch with other configurations of the world in which we live. When the private imagination of the individual predominates, there is always the danger of despair, that is a sense of total aloneness that can overwhelm. As William Lynch sums up: 'What happens in despair is that the private imagination, of which we are so enamoured, reaches the point of the end of inward resource and must put on the imagination of another if it is to find a way out.' (William F. Lynch, *Images of Hope: Imagination as Healer of the Hopeless*, University of Notre Dame Press,

1965:23). Hope, which is really a response to the inner temptation of despair, arises when my little imagination is enlarged by
the imagination of others. Thus the exchange of images, stories
of different accounts of the world, is the catalyst activating the
dynamism of hope. It is only in and through the collaboration,
or mutuality, of imaginations, that hope can emerge and transform the temptation to despair. It is this alternative imaging of
the world by the other that enables hope to transcend the suffo-
cating particularity of one's own private imagination. The imagination that heals the hopeless is the imagination expanded by
interacting with the imaginations of others.

At present the religious imagination is going through a particularly parched period in the history of its existence, and this may
be due to its isolation from the artistic, literary and scientific
imaginations. There is something of an irony in the fact that, at a
time when the religious imagination is in decline, the scientific
imagination is on the increase. The time has come when a new
dialogue between the religious and scientific imaginations
should take place if the much needed transformation of the present eclipse of hope is to take place.

A peep at the scientific imagination
Some will baulk at this new dialogue because the scientific imagination of the modern era did not serve the religious imagination
well. In fact, many would argue that the modern scientific imagination squeezed God out of the world through the mechanisa-
tion of nature and the secularising of the self and society. Is it
possible that some aspects of the post-modern scientific imagination might act as a mid-wife to a revitalisation of the religious
imagination? Let me suggest in mere outline two examples from
the scientific imagination in which this might begin to happen.

The new cosmic story, coming from astrophysics and contemporary cosmologies, is helping humanity to rediscover the fundamental unity of everything in the world, with particular refer-

ence to the exquisite unity that obtains between the cosmos, the earth and the self. This new cosmic story tells us that the human self is the earth and the cosmos in a state of self-conscious freedom. The images of living in 'a finely tuned universe', of being part of 'a cosmic dance', of participating in 'a symphony of life', might well help the religious imagination to discover the meaning of social solidarity, ecological responsibility and interpersonal communion. Religion needs to rediscover these basic ideas if it is to redesign an inclusive theology of hope pertinent to the present and capable at the same time of imaging the future.

A second example might be taken from what the scientific imagination has to say about human origins. Contemporary scientists, in the light of the new story about the evolution of the cosmos, talk about human beings as children of cosmic dust: 'We are all made of the ashes of dead stars.' (J. Polkinghorne, *One World: The Interaction of Science and Theology,* London: SPCK, 1986:56). If the scientific imagination is able to move from cosmic dust to human beings in this way, surely the Christian religious imagination should be able to talk credibly about the transformation of human dust into a new creation in Christ.

Of course there is a radical difference between the imagination of science and the imagination of religion. They deal with different subject matter, different sources of meaning, and different methodologies. Equally important, it must be emphasised, is that religion must resist the temptation of tying its particular insights to any one specific scientific hypothesis. There can be no doubt that current scientific theories will change in the future and, to this extent, theology cannot be tied to any one particular scientific theory. However, these differences between the scientific and religious imagination – and they are significant – will only emerge when the conversation begins. In the meantime, the isolation of the religious imagination needs to be transformed by interaction with the scientific imagination.

One place where this dialogue might take place is in the search for hope in our world today. A productive context in which this search for hope should be made explicit is the month of November in which we honour and remember our dead. By remembering the dead, with hope for them and ourselves, we need the help of the imagination to go beyond the cynicism and apathy that are characteristic of so much politics and religion today.

PART TWO: SAMPLE HOMILIES

DEATH OF AN OLDER PERSON

Self-Surrender

Eltin Griffin O Carm

READING: LK 22:44-49

There is an old Irish story about a tailor in Co Clare. He had a large family and had to work very hard to support them. He didn't have much time for prayer but every time he pierced a piece of cloth and drew the needle he whispered 'O Jesus, pierce with your mercy the hearts of all poor sinners who are going to die in the world today.' Tailoring has advanced a great deal since then. Technology has caught up with it. But it is still a beautiful trade, working on fabric. It requires enormous concentration. It is a very creative work. The master tailor is more than a trades-man. He is a craftsman and an artist. The end product is always distinctive and a work of art. It is not only a creative art; it is also recreating. Allied to a happy home life, it can lead to great con-tentment, composure of spirit and a contemplative outlook on life. It can lead to a very high quality of life and living. However, the greater the quality of life, the harder it is to part with it. We see it in the case of Jesus himself, the struggle that engaged him in Gethsemane when everything seemed a failure in the face of death. The struggle on the cross when he cries out in utter desol-ation 'My God, My God, why have you forsaken me?' There is a hymn which is used in the Mass of Easter Sunday, a sequence which is sung before the gospel, the *Victimae Paschali,* which puts this struggle in a nutshell:
    'Death and life contended
    combat strangely ended.'
Death, let's face it, is disintegration. There is the struggle to part with what is the most precious thing of all, and that is life itself.

And yet, is the most total act of self-surrender, of self-giving. It brings together into one, all the acts of self-giving, of self-surrender, of commitment to the Lord and to others that we have made in this life. Dying, as one French spiritual writer puts it, is one's own little Mass. The church puts on our lips at night prayer, 'Father into your hands I commend my spirit.'

Joe made his final act of self-surrender at 2.05 on Friday last, surrounded by a loving family who had kept vigil with him for several days. But he didn't give up too easily. He had that strength of steel which was part of his stock and trade. He wanted nothing else at his funeral but lots of singing. Such a humble self-effacing man, he would not be a bit too pleased at my eulogising his virtues here this morning. He said to his son before being admitted to the Meath Hospital, 'Face your father's death, son. You will find it the most purifying experience of your life.' What a man of faith!

I have attended many a dying person in my time, but Joe was the first ever to ask me to read a poem for him and he was quite low on that particular day. His favourite poet was Yeats, and one poem he obviously loved was the 'Fiddler of Dooney'. 'You'll find it,' he said to me, 'on page 34.'

When we come at the end of time
To Peter sitting in state
He will smile on the three old spirits
But call me first, through the gate.
For the good are always merry
Save by an evil chance
And the merry love to fiddle
And the merry love to dance
And when the folk there spy me
They will all come up to me
With here is the Fiddler of Dooney
And dance like a wave of the sea.

DEATH OF AN OLDER PERSON

Harvest Time

Aidan Ryan

READINGS: GAL 22-25; LK 8:4-15

In this part of the country, a word that's rarely used is the word 'autumn'. Instead, people refer to the August-October period as 'harvest'. There is an air of fullness and completion about this time of year, an atmosphere that the poet Keats described with the phrase 'mists and mellow fruitfulness'.

Today we celebrate the funeral Mass of TJ in this atmosphere of mellowness, fruitfulness, fullness and completion. We come to give God thanks for a long life, a life filled with the fruits of the Holy Spirit – love, joy, peace, patience, kindness, faithfulness and gentleness – the harvest of a life well lived.

Death is sometimes described in literature, or depicted in art, as the 'Grim Reaper', a kind of skeletal ghost that comes with a sharp scythe to mow us down. But that is not how Christian faith sees death. The Christian vision is much better expressed, I think, in the well-known Irish poem, *Ag Críost an Síol:*

Christ's is the seed and Christ's the harvest.

May we be gathered into God's barn.

Christ sowed the seed of eternal life many years ago in TJ when he was brought as an infant to (this) church for his baptism, or to use the more popular local word, his christening, his first and greatest bonding into union with Christ. In all the years that have passed since then, Christ tended that seed as it grew. He nourished the tender seeds of his young Christian life in his First Confession and Communion and Confirmation. Christ saw that seed come to full bloom in TJ's adult life, in his marriage and his rearing of his family. Christ saw the growth of that seed into a ripe old age. And now, in the fullness of his time, Christ has gathered to himself the rich abundant harvest of a long and fruitful life.

No matter how long a life is, there is still a great sadness in death, especially for those who have to bid even a temporary farewell to a dearly-loved father and grandfather, a good neighbour, a cherished friend. But our faith makes us hopeful today as we look forward to the time when God's harvesting will be complete, and we will all be gathered together with him and with those we have loved, to be happy forever in the kingdom of God's eternal love.

DEATH OF AN OLDER PERSON

'It is a holy and a wholesome thought to pray for the dead'

Brendan McConvery, C.Ss.R.

READINGS: 2 MACC 12:43-45; PS 102;
ROM 6:3-9; MT 25:31-46

Kathleen has gone to join the 'holy souls' whom she always considered as close friends. No rosary was ever said without a prayer for the dead. At every Mass, she had a list of departed friends and neighbours that lengthened with every year that passed. It was not simply a list. Each had a name and a face, and a memory of some act of kindness to be repaid with a prayer. The anniversaries of the family dead were never forgotten. November was her special time. It began at Hallowe'en, as she so often told us of how, when she was young, her granny would bring her to visit the church in the evening of All Saints. Six times the 'Our Father', 'Hail Mary' and 'Glory Be'. Many visits were packed into that half-hour. Then back home in the twilight, the young girl and the old woman, happy in the confidence that their prayers had brought some recently deceased neighbour, or a poor forgotten one with no-one to pray for them, past the ever-vigilant Peter straight to the waiting embrace of Mary and her son.

Kathleen was a quiet and a gentle woman. The only things she probably had in common with the warrior Judas, who was praised in the first reading, is that, like him, in all this, she took full account of the resurrection. She was brought up with unwavering certainty that it was a holy and a wholesome thought to pray for the dead that they may be released from their sins. It was a belief she never lost, and with it went a hope that she would be remembered in the prayers of those she left behind. There was another woman once who had the same sort of faith as Kathleen. The story of her death, written by her son, is one of the most moving pages of Christian writing. He was the great Augustine, she was St Monica. Monica died far from home, but she did not want a lavish funeral. As she told Augustine, who has so often scalded her heart, 'Lay this body wherever it may be. Let no care of it disturb you. This alone do I ask of you, that you remember me at the altar of God.' For Kathleen, the boundary walls between heaven and earth were never very thick, but they were at their thinnest at the time of the celebration of the eucharist. It was truly a moment of living communion of the saints. We are honouring the request in a very special way now, but I think she would want us to remember her always at the altar of God.

Prayer for the dead is deeply ingrained in our Catholic tradition, and expresses in a simple way some of the deepest truths of our faith. It expresses first of all our utter certainty that the faithful departed are in God's sure keeping and that nothing can take them from his hand. It also expresses our confidence in a merciful God who respects our efforts, and does not demand any more of us than we are able to give.

In the gospel, we listened to Matthew's account of the final judgement. St John of the Cross caught the essence of that account when he remarked that 'in the evening of life, we will be judged on love'. The test of love is to have fed the hungry, clothed the naked, to have made a place in our hearts for the forgotten and the rejected. Our education in love began at baptism, when, as St Paul puts it, we were plunged into the mystery of the death and resurrection of Christ. It is a lesson so vital that we spend the rest of our lives learning its truth. Some people are wonderfully quick at picking it up. Most of us, though, have to admit that we are slow learners. We may not be conscious of great sin, but often, there is a meanness, a stinginess and a fear of the cost of being generous, in the love we show to others. Our traditional belief in purgatory sometimes compared it to the familiar experience of a child who has failed in her school-work and has to stay behind to do extra lessons. The time of detention may not last very long, but for the child who wants to play in the sunlight with her friends, every moment can seem like hours. We really do not know how long the lesson of purgatory lasts. It could be simply the moment when, as we enter the presence of the Lord in death, we become aware of just how often and how meanly we have failed, but that all that failure of ours is transformed by the resurrection of Jesus.

DEATH OF AN OLDER PERSON

Going Home

Ambrose Tinsley OSB

READING: JN 14:1-6

'Do not let your hearts be troubled.' These are good words for
such a moment as this. When someone dies, especially a person
who has been a part of our own lives for many, many years, there
is not just a sense of emptiness but also the disturbing presence
of unanswerable questions, even if we do not put them into
words. Our mood is constantly sad, as is the colour of the clothes
we tend to wear. Indeed, if we who come around the altar to con-
celebrate this Mass have chosen purple vestments, rather than
the white ones which are sometimes used, it is because they sym-
bolise the grieving, with so many questions unresolved, which
are inevitable stages of our journey here on earth. And so, we
sympathise in a very special way with Pauline and her family for
whom May has, for so long, meant so much.

They called her Auntie May. Indeed, the first time that I met
her she was getting off a bus to visit Pauline and her family as she
so often did. Their house for May in those days was a second
home and, later, when her own strength was failing, she accepted
their invitation to remain with them. I always found and often
chatted with her there. I consequently know that sometimes she
could feel that she was just a nuisance and a burden, but I also
know that never did she cease to be a loved and valued person in
their home.

But now she has gone to another home. Her going, when it
actually happened, was a quiet, almost unexpected one. The
Hindu people, I am told, refer to death as but the quenching of a
lamp because the dawn has come. May's death was just like that.

It was the silent stopping of a candle flame and she now knows, in a way that we do not, why she does not require it any more. For her the dawn of that new day, the day that shall not ever end, has come. The light which she possesses now is that of Christ himself, the Risen One, and so the warmth and happiness of his eternal home is hers.

Hope But let us come back for a moment to the gospel which we have just heard. It tells us that before his own departure Christ had said to his disciples: 'I am going to prepare a place for you.' He wanted them to know that, after he had left them, he would do all that he could to make it possible for them to follow and to be with him again. Can we now not say the same of May? Has she not gone to share in her own way in that same work of Christ? Is she not now preparing an important place for those who have already done so much for her? I'm sure she is and I am sure that those who loved her in this present life will find that in the life to come one of their very special joys will be enjoying it with her.

Of course we have no adequate idea of what that life, which is ahead of us, is going to be like. The scriptures sometimes speak about it as a meal or banquet to which everyone is called, and sometimes as a paradise in which there will be no more tears or pain of any kind. They also say, and this may be encouraging considering our black or purple clothes, that in our life we will be robed in white. That surely is an image filled with hope, although we still have to admit that the reality will far outstrip what those 'white robes' imply.

However, as we keep on yearning for what is to come, those who knew Auntie May throughout her earthly life have many reasons to be certain that their future is in good and well-experienced hands.

DEATH OF AN OLDER PERSON

The Grain Falls

Benedict Hegarty OP

READINGS: 2 TIM 4:6-8; JN 12:20-26

There can be lives full of possibility that are cut off in their youth. We are left wondering what way they would go; how would things have turned out for them; and we are saddened by all that could have happened and now is lost forever. In the case of our friend (name), it is all different. For her, her days among us were lengths of years and joy. Every indicator says she lived a long, happy and fulfilled life.

She died in the autumn of her life. Each season of the year has its own beauty. Spring has its, with its superabundance of life and growth. Well wrapped up in winter, we can appreciate the trees and bushes glittering with frost; the mantle of snow covering ugliness; the warmth, welcome, comfort of homes. Summer is a tranquil season. It is a time for holidays, slowing down of the tempo of days, long evenings, bright mornings. Autumn has its special beauty. A poet once described it in the following words:

Season of mists and mellow fruitfulness,

Close bosom-friend of the maturing sun.

It is a time of harvest and fruitfulness. The trees look spectacular in their autumn garb.

There is an autumn in life too. The good fight has been fought. Energies are declining but with it comes the shedding of responsibilities and much contentment. Many people shy off from the very thought of it, but the poet had another angle. He could see the riches, the achievement, the colour, the contentment of autumn. That too is the experience of many people as they grow older: they are calm, peaceful, fulfilled, happy, rich in relationships and maturity.

There was something of the autumn with all its special goodness about the last years of (name). There was a basic contentment and peace. There was a sense of duty done, life lived, love given and received.

Autumn signals the end of an age of life. In the flaming forests, life is declining and winter is about to set in. Decline is not the whole story, however. Dead leaves are falling to the ground but they are not alone. The seeds of new life are also falling. Jesus thought of this when he spoke of the grain of wheat. It falls into the ground; it seems to die but in the act of dying and being received into the earth it gives birth to the green sprout, beautiful and bountiful. In the winds and storms of autumn the seeds are shaken from the branches. Sometimes they are caught by a gentle breeze; other times, it is a violent storm that snatches them, whirls them through the air. In the end, they fall to the welcoming earth which is ready to receive them and is life giving. Dying is part of living and a step along the road of on-going life.

When autumn comes in life, it is also difficult to let go. Letting go can be painful and long or short and quick. But having let go, (name) spirit did not flutter off into darkness. Every Sunday we profess our faith in the resurrection of Jesus of Nazareth. In doing so we also proclaim our faith in a new life for every man, woman and child from the beginning to the end of human history. That is our routine faith. The statement of belief is said so often. 'We look for the resurrection of the dead.' It is our everyday faith and then there comes the day when these words take on a deep personal message for us. Such a moment is now when we are laying to rest one whom we knew in our different ways – a parent, spouse, friend, neighbour. Then the words 'we look for the resurrection of the dead' take on a new meaning.

There are many choices to make in life as there are many great events in life. Life ends with the greatest event of all. When we have done everything that God has mapped out for us in the space of life he has given us; when the autumn and harvest of achievement has arrived, then it is time to hand ourselves back to him in a last homecoming.

So it was with (name). In the autumn of her life, she released her spirit to God; was received by his welcoming love and made ready for a new spring in God's life-filled presence forever.

DEATH OF AN OLDER PERSON

Blessing and Faithfulness

Brian McKay O Carm

READINGS: IS 25:6-9; PS 22; REV 21:1-7; JN 14:1-6

We gather in this holy place today to bid farewell to N., to pray for the repose of his soul and to pray for the consolation of those who mourn N.'s passing from this world. Death is always a shock. No matter how inevitable the end may be, we always experience an acute pain when one whom we have loved dearly passes from our midst. At a sad time like this, what can we hold onto that will help to ease the pain?

Firstly, we recall that N. enjoyed a long life and received many blessings and graces from God down through the years. *(Here, mention some points of relevance from the person's life.)* For these blessings, we give thanks and praise to God.

Secondly, we remember N.'s faithfulness. The great virtue in the Old Testament was the virtue of faithfulness, that is, sticking to one's convictions through thick and thin, and this can easily be said of N. His devotion to his family, to his religion which he cherished so much, to his friends, was an example from which we can all learn. Perhaps today he wants us to stop and consider how great our faithfulness to our faith is, how great is our commitment to Our Lord Jesus Christ.

Thirdly, we can be consoled today by our memories of N. Memory is a truly wonderful thing, for at will we can recall incidents and events that make us realise just how special and unique a person N. was. *(Again here it is good to share some appropriate facet of the person's life.)* What is even more wonderful again is the fact that how we remember N. is the way he is in the eternal present of God's presence. It is true to say that for N. time as we know it has stopped for his existence is on a new shore in closer communion with God.

Fourthly, in the Apostles' Creed, which we learned as children and which frequently is recited on Sundays, we read: 'I believe in the communion of saints.' We know that N. was not perfect – which of us is? However, it is part of our faith that, in God's time, N. will join this communion of saints who enjoy the constant vision of God's glory, and that N. will be able to intercede for all those left behind still on their journey of faith. N. will probably never make it into the list of canonised saints, but a saint he will be, finding his true home in heaven for, as today's gospel expresses it, 'in my Father's house there are many rooms'.

Finally, there is much consolation to be had from the beauty of the liturgy itself. In times past, death was something to be greatly feared because of the harshness of a judgemental God. Our liturgy today presents us with the love, mercy and compassion of a kind and caring God. The prophet Isaiah reminds us that the time will come when every tear will be wiped away and when God will gather all his loved ones together to celebrate a great feast. Psalm 22 powerfully acknowledges that God is a loving shepherd who will welcome N. home and who will watch over him for all eternity. In the Book of the Apocalypse, we read that there will be no more death and no more mourning or sadness, and as we have already noted, John's gospel speaks of there being room for all who believe that Jesus Christ is the Way, the Truth and the Life.

Today then, we bid farewell to N. Despite our sense of loss, we face the future with courage and hope, knowing that that is what N. would want us to do. We comfort one another in the sure confidence that for N. life has changed, not ended, as the Preface of the Mass expresses it. We also derive comfort from the conviction that N. is at peace with God.

DEATH OF AN OLDER PERSON

A Vacant Space

Dermot A. Lane

READINGS: WIS 1:1-9; ROM 8:31-35, 37-39; JN 14:1-6

The death of a husband and a father is always a painful experience within the family circle. Even though the person may have been blessed with length of years, the finality of death is always a disturbing and disorientating experience. The death of William S. leaves a vacant space and an empty chair within the family home; his death is also a great loss to the world of music.

Billy S. was a man of great dignity and gentleness – of whom it was once observed, 'He never said a bad word about anyone'. He was a family man, devoted to his wife and children throughout his life. Within that devotion to family there was also his deep love of music. He not only loved music but as a teacher he imparted that love of music to others which of course is the sign of a great teacher.

Billy S. will be sadly missed by many different people: his devoted wife M., his children M., J., and A., the world of music, and his many students.

And so while there is sadness surrounding the death of Billy S., it must be said that there is also a sense of gratitude to God for the full life of this man. Indeed it is the wish of his wife that this funeral liturgy would reflect and express a spirit of thanksgiving to God for the gift and talents of this man: as a husband, as a father, as a musician, and as a great teacher.

In addition to all this, Billy was also a man who took his religion seriously. I have no doubt that his love of music mediated the mystery of God and sustained his deep faith in God. He worshipped regularly here in the parish church at the weekends and went to Mass frequently during the week. He had great devotion to the rosary and it is said that if you dropped him home after a music practice he would turn to the person who had given him a lift and say 'Would you like to come in for a cup of Cocoa and the rosary?'!

In spite of our sadness and deep sense of loss at the departure of Billy, we draw strength and consolation from the readings that have been specially chosen by his family for this funeral liturgy.

Our first reading assures us that the souls of the virtuous are in the hands of God and that they are at peace now. Billy was a virtuous and gentle person in his dealings with others – and so we can be sure that he is at peace now.

Our second reading reminds us that nothing can come between us and the love of God made visible in Christ, not even death itself, because we know that the God, who created us out of love and who redeemed us 'in Christ', is the same God who welcomes us home in death into eternal life.

Our gospel gives us the consoling words of Christ addressed to his own disciples and now addressed to us today at this funeral liturgy: 'Let not your hearts be troubled.' Christ has gone before us and through his experience of death he has opened up the way to eternal life for each and everyone of us. This is the heart of the Christian message and it is the reason why we gather as a community of faith to bury our dead in the memory of Christ Jesus, our Lord and Saviour, Amen.

DEATH OF A YOUNG PERSON

Candyfloss

Richard Sheehy

READING: 2 TIM 4

'I have fought the good fight to the end, I have run the race to the finish, I have kept the faith.' These words of St Paul beautifully sum up Bridget's life, and particularly her last year. Since February, Bridget has lived with and waged a courageous battle against cancer. It's a battle that in the end she lost, but she put up a great fight.

Over these past fourteen months, Bridget had to overcome many hurdles: there was the shock of the initial diagnosis, the prospect of chemotherapy, the side-effects of the treatment, the return of the cancer just when she thought she was getting better, and eventually her being confined to bed.

At each of these setbacks, there were moments for Bridget of doubt, of anger, fear and even despair. Bridget didn't hide her feelings at such moments, but they were always of short duration. What impressed me about her was the way she bounced back so quickly, set herself new goals and got on with the struggle. She could accept the limitations her illness imposed on her and still manage to enjoy life. She never lost her sense of humour, nor her interest in what was going on around her, and she hated to feel that she was being left out of anything. Nothing was allowed to escape her attention. I remember a couple of months ago she wrote a list of questions for the doctor in the hospital. I'm sure he was taken aback to find himself on the receiving end of a rigorous cross-examination.

Bridget's greatest strength in her illness was the love and support of her family. She confided to me on more than one occasion how much this meant to her. Everyone rallied round and gave her constant encouragement. Bridget's room became the focal point in the house. It's a tribute, too, to the kind of person that she was that Bridget had such loyal and devoted friends.

She was conscious of the demands her illness made on her family. At times she could be impatient or irritable, but I know she always regretted it immediately. Home meant everything to her, and she could have wished for nothing more than to spend her final days there surrounded by the people she loved.

Bridget would not want me to eulogise her. I can almost hear her telling me to cut the ... candyfloss! (Only the word she would use would be even more colourful!) But I know she would want me to assure her mother and father, her family and friends, that she is with God and that she is happy.

It's hard to understand why she had to die so young. It is perhaps a consolation to know that Our Lord himself has shared Bridget's experience. For Bridget, as for Jesus himself, the race ended prematurely. As with the life of Our Lord there will always be the feeling that there was so much more Bridget could have done, so much more that life had to offer her, so much more she would have liked to do, if only circumstances had been kinder. It was not to be.

But if we are sad today, there is also much to be thankful for. We are grateful for the life she did have, grateful for all the joy she brought into our lives. For you, her family, there's the comfort of knowing that you were able to show Bridget over the past year just how much you all loved and appreciated her. You knew that time was precious. All that you could have done for her, you did. There are no regrets.

A few weeks ago we celebrated our belief that Christ is risen from the dead and has conquered death. Today we believe that Bridget is sharing in that resurrection:

I am the resurrection and the life.

He who believes in me,
even though he dies,
will live forever;
and whoever lives and believes in me
will never die.

This was Bridget's faith, a faith that was personal but deep. This is the faith that we as a community celebrate in our Mass this morning. It is the faith that comforts us in our sorrow.

Bridget, you fought the good fight to the end. You ran the race to the finish. You kept the faith. May you now enter into the joy of eternal life.

Amen.

DEATH OF A YOUNG PERSON

'He shall not grow old'

Brendan McConvery C.Ss.R.

READINGS: WIS 4:7-15; PS 22; 1 JN 3:14-16; JN 11:32-45

Fewer burdens are heavier than the coffin of your son, your younger brother or your best friend on your shoulder. Our hearts go out today to Liam's family, and to the friends who shared the adventure of his young manhood. In our grief, we have listened as the gospel unfolded the story of another young man's death. John tells us so little about Lazarus and his two sisters that he seems to invite us to read between the lines. In Jesus' time, when marriage at a young age was the norm, a family of two sisters and a brother, with no sign of parents, husbands or wives in the background might lead us to suspect that the main actors in the story were three young unmarried people, doing their best to get on with the business of life. Their chain of dreams and hopes depended on the support of one another. That chain is now cruelly broken by death. They had wanted so desperately for him to get well. Over the weeks of Liam's illness, his family have prayed the words of the message the sisters sent to Jesus, 'Lord, the one you love, the one we love, is sick.' We can understand if their grief finds an echo in Mary's reproach to Jesus, 'Lord, if you had been here, my brother would not have died.'

When someone as young as Liam is taken from us, we ask the question 'why did it have to be him?' The answer to a question like this will not come simply by dint of thinking. It has to be distilled from life's experience, from grief and, above all, from time and memory.

We grieve today that a life full of promise seems to have been cut short. Yet, as the first reading reminds us, life's flourishing

cannot be reckoned by the passing of years alone. A poet, who
was overwhelmed by the thought of so many young lives lost on
the battle-fields of World War I, tried to come to terms with so
much death when peace finally came:

They shall not grow old, as we who are left grow old.

Age shall not weary them, nor the years condemn.

At the rising of the sun and in the morning,

We shall remember them.

(Lawrence Binyon: *For the Fallen*)

For almost eighty years now, those words have brought consolation to the families of the fallen. Jesus believed that through the
illness and death of Lazarus the glory of God would be revealed.
As people who believe in the resurrection, we dare to profess our
faith that the death of this young man will show us, in time,
something of God's glory. In Liam's short life and tragic death,
the Lord may also be gracing us with a glimpse of what eternal
life means.

The English writer Graham Greene lived to be over eighty. In
the last interview he gave, to a journalist who visited him some
months before his death, he was asked whether his Catholic faith
in eternal life made the prospect of death any more welcome.
Greene replied that he found the prospect of a life that simply
went on forever boring. Like most of us, Greene was baffled by
the phrase 'eternal life'. In trying to understand it, he put the
stress on the first word. But 'eternity' is a word too big for our
minds to grasp. The only way we can imagine it is by trying to
imagine time stretching out forever. The liveliest party, the most
exhilarating hiking expedition or rock-concert which goes on
too long, ends up by becoming boring. It might be easier to
pierce the mystery of eternal life by beginning with the word
'life'. When we think of Liam at his best, we think of a young
man brimming over with irrepressible energy, with promise,
with laughter. He was someone who never lost the capacity to
surprise us. He was never predictable. That did not make him

always the easiest person to live with. God has taken him to himself at the time when he was most full of life. He will be forever fixed in our memory and in our hearts as someone who was not crushed by the burdens of life, even by his last illness. He was not made cynical by dreams which never fulfilled their promise, or made cautious by bitter experience. That may be his parting gift to us, a reminder that life is exuberant, and ever youthful. If it is eternal, then it will be ever new, ever full of surprises, bursting with a promise that there is more to come.

Soon we shall carry the body of Liam, washed with holy water and perfumed with incense, to its final resting place. There we will confide him to the care of the Lord who wept by the tomb of Lazarus his friend. Let us do it in the hope of the final words, 'Unbind him, and let him go free'.

DEATH OF A YOUNG PERSON

Wholeness and Holiness

Brian McKay O Carm

READINGS: WIS 4:7-15; PS 22; THESS 4:13-18; MT 11:25-30

The news of N.'s death was a message which shocked and saddened all who knew N. We could scarcely believe it then – we
can scarcely believe it now. We have lost a valued and loved
member of our community and, really, we are trying to make
sense of an aspect of human life which is so difficult to understand. We do not know why God has taken N. at this young age
and, probably, we will never comprehend it this side of the grave.
Today, we need to ask ourselves if there is anything that we can
hold onto to help us through this time of grief, something to
help us cope with the feeling of darkness, the feeling of a bright
light having been extinguished.

There is the memory of N. himself, his personality, his talents, his achievements, the gift that he was to his family, to his
friends, to his school (university, job) and to his local community.
(Here it is good to make direct reference to the person's life.) For N.
was a gift who helped spread God's love everywhere he went during his short life, and for the gift of this young person, we give
thanks and praise to God. We are all the better for ever having
known him.

Our gospel today extends an invitation to each one of us to
'come to me, all you who labour and are overburdened and I will
give you rest'. God wanted N. to be nearer to him and now we
believe that N. is being taken care of. We who are left behind
must take care of each other and, in so doing, God's healing
power will be at work among us to give us strength, consolation,
and courage for the future. Remembering N., his good points,

his weaknesses, his talents, his personality, will be very important for everyone over the next few weeks and months. The memory of a person no longer with us can be a very powerful aid to our coping with a distressing and inexplicable situation. The memory of a person can help us to get on with our own lives as, indeed, we must.

Those of us left behind may also need to learn something from N.'s life and death. N.'s passing from us may show us that life is a gift, something very precious, something that each of us should value and cherish. Sometimes, we need to be reminded that life is good and worth putting effort into. Perhaps that is a message that N. would like us to hear today.

Our liturgy provides us with words of hope today. The Book of Wisdom reminds us that N. achieved perfection or wholeness in a short time and, so, was ready to enter into the presence of God. It is no accident that the words wholeness and holiness are so close. N. has now achieved both. The gospel consoles us by giving us to understand that N. now knows many things about the kingdom of God and therefore is very close to God.

There is something else to hold onto today. On Sundays at Mass we speak the words 'we believe in the communion of saints'. It is part of our faith that N. has now joined the communion of saints and, as such, is of great benefit to us all. You know that in Catholic spirituality it is quite common to pray for some favour through the intercession of a saint. As a member of this great number of blessed people, N. is now in a position to intercede on behalf of his parents, family and friends and so help them in a new and powerful way. N. we believe has now achieved perfection himself and can help those left behind to do likewise.

I wonder what message N. would like to impart to us today as he keeps an eye on our doings. I think he would want us all to be strong, determined, unafraid of the future, ready to meet every challenge – to believe in ourselves and to try and keep believing in God, even if that seems to be difficult at this time.

Finally, we wish again to extend our deepest sympathy to all N.'s family and friends. We know that these days are most traumatic. By our presence we want to say to you that we are grieving with you and will do all we can to support you over the next few days, weeks, months. The Lord Jesus says, 'I am the resurrection and the life. If anyone believes in me, even though he dies, yet will he live.' N. is with God; N. is at peace.

DEATH OF A YOUNG PERSON

'They have taken (my Lord) away'

Betty Maher

READING: JN 19:25-27

As we face the sorrow and loneliness of today, and of the days and weeks and months ahead, perhaps – not now, but a little later – we may find some comfort in remembering that on the day of Jesus' death, Mary, too, knew the kind of pain which (we) are experiencing here today. There were more than three crucifixions on that day, because no mother could stand below the cross of her child and not feel that she herself was being crucified.

Jesus, like all of us when we are in physical pain, must have felt his own suffering. And therefore, as I see it, it was an extraordinary example of human love and pity – pity in the best sense of the word – that moved Jesus to become aware of the pain of his mother who stood alongside him, and to momentarily forget his own pain, in order to look for some way in which he could ease that pain for her.

For us here today, there is just such pain, and there are also questions. (Even though we may have known that N.'s death was expected, we are still left with questions.)

But when someone dies who is young – a baby, or someone who is living a full and busy life, with youth and beauty on their side, and is suddenly and inexplicably cut down – then the questions seem to multiply.

Jesus, too, died in the prime of life; and Mary was his mother. How could she hope to understand what was happening? Is there any way to deal with this sort of shock, and the pain attached? I think that to find a fitting answer one would have to be God.

At the very time when he was suffering most, Jesus, in the fullness and vulnerability of his humanity, must have felt as inadequate as many of us no doubt do today. He was looking at his grieving mother, and was unable to take her pain away. So too, we are helpless, in the face of death, to 'make it all right'.

And so Jesus did the best he could manage; he looked for a way in which his mother's future life might in some way be eased. (One interpretation I have read of this story suggests that just as Mary influenced the early years of Jesus and gave him direction, so now he gave her direction for her future life – life without him – just when it must have seemed to her that, as his life's blood drained away, so did hers also.)

And for this he needed the co-operation of his friend. And he got it. John's response to Jesus when he was asked to look after Mary, must have been a real chink of light for Jesus himself at that moment, as he neared his last breath.

Although his own pain was drawing to an end, Jesus knew that Mary would have to endure. In the natural order of things she would not have seen his death. He was facing the loneliness of death by himself, and he knew that she would have to do the same, as all of us must. This, I believe, adds to the pain of everyone when someone they love dies. It is the loneliness of the human condition.

But this is also, I like to think, the very reason why we can hope; we can surely hope that some day such loneliness will finally be over, and we will experience re-union in love.

And so, today, just as Mary went as far as she could with her dying son, so we too can only try to walk with one another, and especially with those whose loss is greatest. We will feel inadequate, that's for sure, but by sharing in so far as we can the pain of those who most deeply mourn, we can try our best to 'be Christ' to one another. Our inadequacy, our sheer human clumsiness, is part of being human, I am sure – but it is well to remember too that this very lack is part of the reason why we can continue to hope; to hope that a time will come, for all of us, when such inadequacies will be no more.

Mary's faith and love saw her through the crucifixion of her only child. As we move along this lonely road today, let us pray for one another, that we will find in the love of those nearest to us the love and support which Jesus asked of John towards his mother, and which he also asked of Mary towards the Beloved Disciple.

DEATH OF A YOUNG PERSON

Have no fear

John Wall

READINGS: WIS 4:7-15; PS 48 1-13; 2 COR 5:1; 6-10; MT 25:31-40

When Mother Teresa of Calcutta used to quote that gospel, as she did frequently, it seemed to make a lot of sense to a lot of people – even to those who were not, as we might put it, 'big into' religion. It simply says that at the end of the day we're judged on love, on how we treated each other. For that reason Brian need have no fear as he goes before his God. His life was built on love. And he, in turn, was – and is – greatly loved himself.

This Mass is a sad occasion for all of us. It is also a 'eucharist', a celebration of thanksgiving for Brian's life. And there is much to be grateful for. Last evening I talked to Brian's mother and father and his family and together we prepared this liturgy. As they spoke, I was struck by the amount of echoes of today's gospel, of goodness to other people, that were evident in his life. I'm sure each one of you here will have had your own memories of Brian as you have sat and swapped your own stories, as people do at times like this.

He packed so much into his short life. As our first reading put it: 'Being perfected in a short time, he fulfilled long years, for his soul was pleasing to the Lord'.

As with most young people, music was very important in his life. Brian would go along with the response to our Psalm today: 'I will solve my problem with the harp', or in his case, with his guitar. We saw that guitar, along with other personal reminders of Brian, carried in the Entrance Procession at the beginning of our liturgy. I think we can begin to take in the *big* fact of death slowly as an inevitable natural fact of life. But isn't it true to say that it's those *small* things that make our tears flow? And tears are healthy and natural. Jesus himself wept at the death of his good friend Lazarus.

Bereavement is the price of love. When a person is greatly loved then that person will be greatly missed. So at times like this we have a great need of love and kindness and concern and a rallying around of friends – just as we have seen happen here since the news of Brian's death.

It may be usual for the children to be present at the funeral of a parent. But it goes against the normal run of life for a parent to bury a child. So our hearts go out especially today to Brian's Mam and Dad. We pray that not alone will they have the consolation of a pride in a wonderful son and of a united family – which we all have witnessed over the past few days – but also the consolation of their faith, of knowing that Brian is now beyond all pain and suffering and has gone home to God our Father – to inherit the kingdom prepared for him – and for all of us – 'since the foundation of the world'.

There are a lot of young people here this morning, as there were last evening when Brian's funeral came to the church. For many of you, this will be your first experience of the death of someone in your *own* age group. You may even be closer to the altar today than you would be on an average Sunday. The speed of life does not usually allow you much time for long prayers or deep meditation. But today we are stopped in our tracks, trying to get our heads around the big questions, like: 'What's it all about?' The second Reading may point towards an answer: 'We are always of good courage ... for we walk by *faith*, not by sight'.

Brian wasn't rich – but he left a legacy. In fact he left a *treasury*, a treasury of love. It seems that since he died that treasury has been opened. All of us around here have shared in it. We have experienced it in the coming together of friends, neighbours reaching out to each other, people wanting to help in any way they can, wonderful acts of kindness, the gospel of coming to life.

People in mourning often ask: 'What can I do with all this love now that my friend has gone?' The best tribute, the best memorial, that we can have to Brian is to use that legacy of love. Giving it especially to those who need it most. 'As long as you did it to one of these, the least of my brothers and sisters, you did it to me.'

That's what the Lord wants of us and that's what Brian did. And we thank God for the sheer simplicity of his example of gospel living and giving in his young life. May he rest in peace.

DEATH OF A YOUNG PERSON

To Grieve With Hope

Dick Lyng OSA

READINGS: WIS 4:7-15; ROM 8:14-18; MK 15:33-39

[handwritten: THIS DEATH OF JESUS ON THE CROSS]

The funeral Mass functions at many levels. We have gathered first of all to pray for Rory, that his soul may now find rest in God. We gather here also to offer our support to the Kavanagh family, to Rory's heartbroken parents, Des and Mary, to his brothers Ronan and Conal, to his girlfriend of five years, Colette. Through our presence here in such great numbers, we are stating publicly that we too recognise the blessing that Rory was. We are expressing gratitude to the Kavanagh family for moulding Rory into that charming young man that he was, and for sharing him with the rest of us.

In the funeral Mass too we strive to come to terms with reality, to face head-on the loss we have suffered, to peer into the heart of this dark mystery and to cry out in the words of the writer Joseph Conrad: 'The horror, *The horror, The horror'.* The funeral Mass should never be viewed as an escape from grief or a denial of death. Rather, the funeral Mass teaches us to inhabit this darkness and to grieve with hope. The Kavanagh family will identify with that Calvary scene from Mark's gospel and they will make their own the despairing cry of the dying Christ: 'My God, My God, why have you abandoned us?'

But we will never come to terms with this grief unless we first savour the enormity of our loss. Even the loss of an elderly relative can be experienced as a cruel blow. The severing of old bonds can be painful. They are our own flesh and blood. With their death dies part of us. Pain seems to be the price that love demands. This is the law of life, the ordinary course of events.

How much more painful then, how much more cruel, is the loss of a young life in tragic circumstances. The human reaction is one of numb disbelief. The Kavanagh family have been to hell and back several times since Sunday last. Their worst nightmare has conspired to overwhelm them. Their loss is acute only because they loved Rory dearly. An outgoing, vivacious, affectionate young man, he resisted the constraints of convention and location.

Rory was a wandering spirit, intellectually, artistically and physically. He loved Italy. The spontaneity of the Mediterranean life appealed to him greatly. After completing his BA he dabbled professionally and successfully in the music business for a year. At the time of his death he was working in the computer business but, by all accounts, his ear and mind began to turn again to his first love, music. But, unfortunately, that dream remains unrealised. Rory would have understood perfectly the words of our first reading: 'Length of days is not what makes age honourable, nor number of years the true measure of life.' Life was a gift to be explored and celebrated. And, for him, the highest expression of that celebration was to be found in music.

Nine months ago, Rory was given a warning. A minor heart condition made him medically vulnerable. An alteration of lifestyle was called for. He was warned to cut back on his socialising and take regular exercise. He was scared by this warning and he took it seriously for a time. But, as often happens, time deprived that warning of its original sting. The impatience of youth reasserted itself. Rory must have concluded that the safe, conventional life could best be lived by those who were good at it. His young life was snuffed out by that fatal flaw on Sunday morning last.

In the days and months ahead, Des and Mary, Ronan, Conal and Colette will labour under a black cloud of grief. They will cling to treasured memories of Rory. As Des confessed, Rory inherited his good looks from Mary and his mischievous humour from Des. They will remember above all the affectionate centre of a very close family, a beaming smile that lit up their lives. They will carry with them too some consoling memories from these dark days. They will treasure the outpouring of affection and grief from his great host of friends and peers. They will never forget that you stood shoulder to shoulder with them and held their hand as they stumbled blindly through this valley of darkness. To paraphrase the poet T.S. Eliot, 'These fragments they have shored against their ruin.' But their strongest support will come from their Christian faith which I know has always been central to their lives and to the gentle way they live out their lives. They will draw strength from the knowledge that the God they worship has walked this dark path before them.

May Rory now find rest in God.

DEATH OF A YOUNG PERSON

The Silence of God

Richard Sheehy

READINGS: WIS 4:7-15; LK 24:13-35

When someone dies, we have a need to try to express what that person meant to us, what we feel they were about. Keara's friends and classmates have spoken very warmly and movingly of the young woman they knew. They have captured in little vignettes, something of her rich personality.

When we highlight in retrospect what we admired in a person like Keara – her talents, her charm, her sense of purpose, her pursuit of excellence, her discipline, her sensitivity to others, her sense of fun, her independence of mind, her freedom of spirit, her depth, her beliefs – we are not trying to eulogise her beyond recognition. She would chide us for making her into a saint. Keara had her faults and weaknesses and would be the first to acknowledge them. She was not everybody's closest friend, but she was universally respected and admired. She was her own person.

But in recalling her qualities, we are, in fact, describing ideals and values that we are attracted to and hold deep down – perhaps without even being aware of it. They are values that we consider important, goals that we are inwardly striving towards. We are touching into a deeper truth: that God gave us life, that our lives have purpose, and our task is to discover and pursue that purpose.

We want our lives to have meaning, to make a difference. We are not content to merely exist, to drift along enjoying life, to consume. Whatever our chosen branch of study or work here in college, most of us are not just in it to get a degree, or hopefully a job. We want to participate in the task of creating a more caring, compassionate, equitable and open society, to make life more human for others; in effect, to realise the kingdom of God. St Augustine said: 'We were made for union with you; and our hearts are restless, until they rest in you.' I know that Keara cared about other people – their aspirations and needs. It came through in her involvement in the college St Vincent de Paul Society, particularly with the Sunday 'hikes' for local children.

When Ignatius Loyola had to lie for months in a hospital bed, recovering from his war wounds, he used to dream about the great things he would do in the future, once he was well again (modelling himself on the lives of the saints he was reading about). It's good to dream, to imagine the world differently, but the future begins today, not tomorrow. More important than the things we plan to do in the future once we are qualified and have our degree, is allowing our dreams to shape the way we live now.

Keara had dreams, but she wasn't the kind to sit around waiting for things to happen. She pursued her goals and made personal sacrifices to make them happen, be it in the area of athletics, academic endeavour or more personal achievements. As one of her friends remarked earlier, Keara wasted no time. She lived life fully, making the most of the present moment. The wise author of our first reading suggests that it's not how long we live that is significant, but rather *how* we live. What's important is not which gifts we have or don't have, but rather our willingness to develop and use the ones we do have.

So often we get caught up in the mundane tasks and deadlines of today, that we lose sight of where we are heading. Keara's death stops us in our tracks and causes us to question again what is of ultimate value. We remember Keara today, not to be sad but to draw strength, comfort and inspiration from all that she was and all that she packed into her short life. She would want us to encourage one another to embrace life as she did.

The disciples walking on the road to Emmaus thought that they were alone in their grief and could see only the tragic in what had taken place in Jerusalem. They wondered where God was – he seemed to have let them down. When Jesus walked with them and listened to their pain and loss, he helped them to gain a new perspective on all that had happened, and they realised that God was with them.

Keara's death, in the fullness of her youth and vitality and with so much ahead of her, is devastating. Michael and Gretta have lost a dear daughter; Fergal and Ronan, a beloved sister. We are at a loss to understand why such a freak accident should happen. We can feel let down, abandoned by God. However, another verse in the Book of Wisdom tells us: 'Death was not God's doing, he takes no pleasure in the extinction of the living. To be – for this he created all.'

Cardinal Martini, Archbishop of Milan, spoke of the silence of God in the face of human suffering. Sometimes silence is the only appropriate response to human tragedy, but it's silence charged with love and compassion. Good has already begun to emerge out of this experience of pain and loss. Keara's family have received much support, from their friends and neighbours and from Keara's classmates and friends. Students have been more sensitive to one another and have drawn closer together. The time, enthusiasm and commitment that went into organising today's memorial service speaks for itself.

My prayer is that the memory of how rich Keara's life was, of how deeply she touched the lives of so many people, and of how generous she was in death, may help bring healing, consolation and pride to her family.

For Christians, the real meaning of death is revealed, not on Good Friday, but on Easter Sunday. I have a vivid memory of the day we said goodbye to Keara in Collooney … Just as her coffin was being lowered into the ground, a bright sun appeared unexpectedly from behind dark November clouds and shone warmly on our faces. It seemed to point to another sun, the sun which rose on the morning of the Third Day.

DEATH OF A YOUNG PERSON

Not Measured by Years

Benedict Hegarty OP

READINGS: WIS 4:7-13; JN 11:17-27

This church has seen many funerals – all of them sad, some of them tragic. There is a special tragedy in the death of a young person. There is nothing we can say or think or do that can measure up to the loss of her family. This young person was in our midst. Like all young people she rejoiced in life, looked confidently to the years that lay ahead, dreamed of the way things might be. Now she is asleep. At a moment like this, the evident grief which clutches young and old alike testifies to a people's sense of loss and their loving support for this family.

There is only one prayer in the hearts of those who loved (name). There is only one question in their minds. Could we not have her back? Could these extraordinary and unbelievable days be wiped out? Could we awake from this nightmare? On two occasions, the gospels mention that Jesus wept. In both cases, it was the death of a young person – at the funeral of the widow's son and by the tomb of that young man Lazarus.

All we can offer, now, is a sense of shared loss, a touch of comfort, an assurance of love. Anything else we can do or say is sadly inadequate. Every death is tragic but the death of a young person touches a whole community. There is the loss of a young life; there is the well-up of sympathy within us for the family who mourn. There is a special sympathy – a special love, a special feeling – for the mother and father, the sisters, brothers, the close relatives and friends of (name).

The words of the first reading were penned by someone a long time ago, two thousand years ago and more. He wrote them, obviously trying to cope with a tragedy very like what we have seen over the past few days. He wrote these words helped by God for our comfort this morning. Remember them again. 'The good person, though she die before her time, will find rest. For the age that is honourable comes not with the passing of time, nor can it be measured in terms of years. Young or old, it is understanding that is maturity; a good life this is fulfilment.' We measure life so often by the number of years and its duration. Let's forget about numbers and length; let's think more of accomplishment. Think not of what (name) could have done or would have made of her life; think rather of all she had done and the light and love she left behind.

It was a short life she lived – but then what life is long? It is just that some lives are a little shorter than others. When we go out into the country and see the ruins of cottages and the marks of little fields, we might dream of those who lived there, who played, cared, loved, grew up and died long hence. Life is very short for everyone.

Life is very short. However, a tragic death like this teaches us suddenly and painfully something deeply true. Life, too, is important. There would be no such sense of loss and grief unless we suddenly saw that life is very precious. When a life is torn away from us, then we see that our friends, people, life are all that matter.

We don't know why she had to go to Jesus so soon. A prayer in the liturgy to receive the remains has the words: 'Now in his wisdom, he has called her to himself.' We do not know what this wisdom is. We cannot trace its logic, its thoughts and purposes and answer the question 'why?' For us who believe, we only know that plan and wisdom is there and one day its truth will open to our uncomprehending eyes.

And it is not as if it has all ended. Her life has just taken a different shape and a different form. She and her family were deeply believing and they were so truly right. It is not as if they lost her;

it is just that she is with them in a different way. A few days ago, God said: '(name) I have always loved you from the first moments of your life. Welcome home! You are no further from your mother and father and brothers and friends than I am, and I am so close to you all.'

DEATH OF A YOUNG PERSON

In the light and darkness of life

Dermot A. Lane

READINGS: WIS 4:7-15; 2 COR 5:1-4; JN 11:17-21

The experience of death is always disturbing, but the death of a young person in the prime of life is overwhelming in its effects: it raises unanswerable questions, it challenges the very meaning and purpose of life, and it taxes our faith.

The sudden and tragic death of R. has stunned and shocked all of us gathered here this morning. In particular, the sudden departure of R. has created a deep void in the lives of G. and B., her parents, and in the life of K., her dear brother.

As we all know, R. was a unique and extraordinary young girl, full of life and vitality, gentle in her relationships with others, gifted with a great sense of humour, always sensitive and attentive to the needs of others. R. was someone who touched the lives of others in so many different ways.

She was more than just a daughter to G. and B., she was also a friend and a companion. Likewise R. was more than just a sister to K., she was a trusted pal.

There is something inconsolable about parents having to bury a child, especially a mother having to lay to rest her daughter. This sad experience is something that goes against the grain of nature and the rhythm of life itself.

In trying to come to grips with this untimely death of R., it is as well to acknowledge that there are no easy answers, that there is no cheap consolation in the face of death, that there are no satisfactory sound bites to soften the pain of loss. Pious platitudes ring hollow on occasions like these.

As we mourn the death of R. today, it must be said that it is a futile and empty exercise to speculate about what might have been if R. had not gone to Germany. What is much more important for us is to know that she was extremely happy during her last couple of weeks in Germany, that she wrote and phoned home regularly, sharing that happiness with her family. R. lived life to the full and died living life to the full and doing what she loved to do, namely horse riding and travelling and getting to know new people.

Likewise it is also a futile and empty spirituality that might blame God for this sad and tragic accident. It is not the will of God that R. should have been snatched prematurely from life in this disturbing way.

Instead, what is important for us is to realise that in these tragic circumstances God does not abandon us in our sadness and loneliness. To the contrary, God is with us both in the light and darkness of life, in the joys and sorrows, just as God was with Jesus in life and in death. This is the message that comes across in our readings that have been chosen by G. and B. and K. for this sad occasion.

In our first reading, we are reminded that it is not length of days that make a life honourable but the way we have sought to please God. R. sought to please God in her love of others.

Our second reading assures us that when the earthly tent we inhabit is destroyed, namely when this frail and fragile body that we live in is destroyed by accident or illness or age, then God will give us a new body, everlasting home and dwelling place in heaven – an eternal home where one day we shall all be reunited 'in Christ' when every tear shall be wiped away, and there shall be no more pain, no more mourning (Apoc 20:1-5).

The foundation of our hope in this vision of life is given to us in our gospel reading in the words of Jesus: 'I am the resurrection and the life. He who believes in me, though he die, yet shall he live and whoever lives and believes in me shall never die.' These words of Jesus, addressed to Martha to console her over the death of Lazarus, are also addressed to us here today to console us in our loss of R. They assure us that death is not the end but the beginning of new life, that death is not a slipping away into nothingness but rather a recreation unto eternal life with God. But most of all, these words of Jesus assure us that death is a gathering up of our personal life into God and a gathering into the assembly of God's people, into eternal communion with all who have gone before us through the power of the resurrection of Christ.

And so the sadness and loss of today gradually turns into a sense of gratitude for the life of R. With G. and B. and K., we thank God for the gift and grace of R., for the friendliness and cheerfulness that she shared with others, for the humour and warmth of her relationship with others.

And in the end we pray that each and every one of us, having loved R. here on earth, may continue to love her in eternity. Amen.

DEATH OF A CHILD

Into Your Hands

Aidan Ryan

READINGS: LAM 3:17-26; MT 27:45-50

This church, over the years of its history, has seen many sad and tragic funerals. But few can have been as profoundly sad and sorrowful as the funeral that gathers us here today. The death of a child, in any circumstances, is an occasion of great sorrow. But a death that is the result of a freak and avoidable accident, simply beggars our understanding. While our lips pray the words of faith in the funeral liturgy, our hearts cry out in baffled bewilderment – what kind of a God could allow a young and innocent child to be snatched so cruelly from a loving and devoted family? Does he care? Is he there at all?

Well, I have no easy answers to these questions. All we can do is look at the figure of the crucified Christ and remember his words on the cross: 'My God, my God, why have you forsaken me?' We can understand and identify with the desolate and despairing cry of the crucified Christ on the dark hill of Calvary. Like him, we feel abandoned and forgotten by God in our pain and suffering. And yet the truth, the gospel truth, is that God had not abandoned him, and neither has he abandoned us. Jesus began to see the faintest glimmer of that truth in the final moments of his life as he prayed: 'Father, into your hands I commend my spirit.' The grace we seek from God here today is the grace to be able to make that prayer of Jesus our own as we commend our troubled and tortured spirits into God's loving hands. It takes a long time to travel the journey from 'Why have you forsaken us?' to 'Into your hands we commend our spirits.' It's a journey that can't be rushed. For Joe's parents and his family, it

may take years, it may take a lifetime. We are here as their neighbours and friends as they take their first painful steps along that
road. We are here to stand with them in silent solidarity in the
shadow of this immense cross.

In the Opening Prayer of this Mass, we prayed 'though he was
with us for so short a time, may he live, radiant and forever
young in the kingdom of your love'. Despite the darkness of this
tragedy, our faith teaches us that the destination God has in store
for Joe is just that – radiance and eternal youth in the kingdom
of his love, where we can hope to see him again and be happy
with him forever. For now, we continue to walk in the valley of
tragic and untimely death. But we trust that Christ the Good
Shepherd, who himself knew the darkness of Calvary, will in the
end lead us into the bright joy of Easter morning, where ever tear
will be wiped away. On that day, we shall see you, our God, as
you are and be happy with Joe and with you forever in heaven.

*LET NOT YOUR HEARTS BE TROUBLED - TRUST IN GOD
BELIEVE ALSO IN ME

DEATH OF A PARENT

A New Kind of Belonging

Niall Ahern

READING: JN 14:1-6 *

The death of a parent brings a new kind of unbelonging into a person's life. Before such a death, we were someone's son or daughter but now we are orphaned. Even an adult can be orphaned. To be without a parent is to be in a place of unbelonging.

SHOULD BE

And that's understandable. For one's parent is really one's first friend. One's longest first friend. No friend we will ever meet on life's journey will have been so interested or committed to us. No other friend will have known our first step or our first smile or our first tear. No other friend will know us through and through in such an intimate manner as to be called by our name – a name they themselves have chosen and given us. A parent is one who calls us by name for the first time.

Such uprootedness brings deep pain. We have to redefine ourselves. We have to re-identify ourselves. Going from the place of being known through and through to a search for a new kind of identity is always painful. The loss is something we never get over. On this day of bidding farewell to a parent, there is a certain truth in saying we will never get over it. There is a certain truth in saying that life will never be the same again. And somehow we know in our heart's core that it is good to acknowledge that life will never be the same again; that there won't be the same kind of security; that there won't be the same depth of loving; that there won't be the same sureness of identity. One's parent and their loving of us are synonymous, and both have died today. So where, or to whom, do we now belong?

Someone once said to me that the only other word they could

but here on earth homes are built up by parents. They are the first creators of home. They create the safe place for us – the safe place to be born, to take initiative, to believe, to start the journey of loving. They are the heart of our home. Home, we all know, is where the heart is, and today the heart is not at home. The heart is gone from this place to a different space. For it is true that today home is joined to heaven in a more profound way. The one we love has gone before us to our eternal home. And it is our home too; the ultimate togetherness; where no separation or darkness or parting will ever happen again.

The parent who has just died has joined the host of heaven; the communion of saints; the family of God. Any apartness they may have experienced in life is now transformed beyond loneliness. We honestly are not sure what heaven is really like, it's beyond our imagining; it's our very best thought; our most carefully parcelled gift; our longings all fulfilled. And so however sad and torn apart we are, we couldn't possibly want our parent back today. Maybe for our own sake – yes. But for their sake – no.

Go gently dear Mum. Go gently to a rest beyond words. And may something of your new joy translate itself in time in our regard. We wait in eager longing and with one ray of hope amidst our running tears. And that ray shines out – hope. It brightens our darkness and guarantees our belonging with you always. That ray speaks to us in your name now and tells us how cherished we are by you forever. In your name it whispers: 'Cherish everything of my care for you. Cherish my parenting of you, with all its fondest moments; its intimacy; its closeness. Cherish these and hand them on so that I might parent my children's children. Love is eternal and I'm here to welcome you to your eternal home. And so I say to you, my forever child, we will meet again on God's mountain top in an embrace that will last forever. For together we belong and together we will be in the home of heaven. For this day brings for me, and for you, a new kind of belonging.' Amen.

(13)

[handwritten:] You Are The Salt of the Earth, But if Salt has Lost Its Saltiness...
You Are The Light of The World. A City set on a hill Cannot Be Hid (14)
Nor Do Men Light a Lamp and Put it under a Bushel (15)
Let Your Light so Shine Before Men. That They May See
Your Good Works And Give Glory To Your Father Who is in Heaven.

SAMPLE HOMILIES   89

DEATH OF A PARENT

'When the sun goes down'

Martin Delaney

READING: MT 5:13-16

It was one of those uniquely beautiful days that we sometimes get in late October or early November. Even though it was cold and crisp, the sun shone brightly for most of my long car journey from Kerry to Dublin. Evening was approaching as I entered the final phase of my journey, and I noticed that the magnificent sunshine which had been my loving companion on this day's journey was now about to leave me. Dusk descended quickly and then, in my rear-view mirror, I noticed a curious object in the sky. At first I was not sure what it was, and then I realised it was the moon tentatively making it's faintest appearance. Meanwhile my friend the sun, which had lit up so many of the faces I had seen on my journey today, continued with its inevitable departure. However, my heart got a little lift when I noticed that, as the sun dipped lower in the sky, the moon behind me became brighter and brighter. When the sun finally disappeared, the moon majestically took its place as the brightest object in the sky.

During the final leg of my journey I reflected on the beautiful transition I had just witnessed. I realised that the moon was simply reflecting the light of the sun, now hidden from me. Somehow the moon was continuing the work of the sun. In some real way the moon assured me that the sun lived on eternally and continued to brighten up my life. _[handwritten margin: Funeral Times of Transition]_

Today, as we say goodbye to N., a much loved mother, I am reminded again of that journey from Kerry to Dublin and the reflection I had as the sun went down only to be replaced by the different light of the moon. Like so many parents, N. lived her life like the sun. She brought light and warmth into the lives of her family. She was the source and sustainer of your lives. In the warmth of her embrace, all of you, her children and grandchildren, were empowered and enlightened. From your mother you received incredible gifts, and the energy to develop those gifts for the good of others. In her light was also reflected the light of her God, the love and compassion of God. *(The preacher could elaborate here a little on the particular life and gifts of the deceased.)*

DEATH OF A PARENT

Struggling to see

Michael Paul Gallagher SJ

Do NOT LET YOUR HEARTS

READING: JN 14:1-6; 19-20 — Honoury Minutow.

I last spoke to Kathleen on Thursday afternoon. I phoned her in hospital to know if she was able for a visit. She was in great form because they had just told her she could go home for the weekend of her birthday. So we decided it was much better for me to visit her at home on Sunday. It would be, or would have been, her 59th birthday. But I never saw her again alive because, as we all know, Kathleen died in her own bed, in her sleep, that Saturday night. Sunday became her birthday in another sense, in the Christian sense of being born into a different life with God.

Today, of course, we think of her. Our minds are confused: I myself feel numb with sadness, and yet I remember so much that is good, happy, healing. We were childhood friends and have remained so all these years. We think of Kathleen, painfully because she is gone, but prayerfully and gratefully, because she lived a marvellously full and generous life as wife, mother, grandmother, and as nurse. But perhaps we think even more, in this church this morning, of Paul and of their three children. For such a happy family this is a huge loss, and we simply don't know what to say. But this overflowing church is itself a powerful word of sympathy, which means feeling pain with, sharing the suffering. To all Kathleen's family, our presence here in such numbers is like poetry without words. Because we have no real words worthy of how we feel, worthy of what we might want to say.

Over these short months after Kathleen discovered her illness, she did not have words either. Or else the words she found seldom did justice to her depth. I remember her total shock and anger at the beginning. Anger especially with God. In a friendly but tough way, she took it out on me a few times. 'What kind of God would do this to me? I don't know if I believe anything any-more.' And for weeks she wouldn't receive communion in the hospital when they came round in the early morning. And I had no easy answers. She even teased me about it. 'You're meant to be an expert, and you've nothing to say to me.' Then one day I said something utterly simple and without much thought behind it. I know it reached her because she repeated it to many of her visitors – and so it came back to me! I told her to forget about God and to remember only Jesus. It might sound heretical but, in fact, the word 'God' has strange echoes of distance and power. But the person of Jesus rings so differently, not distance and power, but the opposite: closeness and weakness. Weakness with us. Espec-ially in his own confusion and fear in the garden facing death.

Somehow that little sentence made a difference to Kathleen. She went back to receiving communion. And, these last weeks, panic seemed to give way to a kind of serenity. It was as if she was no longer fighting to win against death, only to lose generously, so to speak. She wanted to leave a sense of peace behind her. As if she wanted to nurse people into what she had discovered with such difficulty – a vision of goodness in spite of the darkness.

Forget about 'God' – in quotation marks. Focus on Jesus Christ. In this spirit, let us turn again to those gospel words spo-ken by Jesus at his Last Supper, words intended to comfort his friends at the idea of his departure.

'Trust in me,' he says, 'I am the Way,' and he adds, 'the world will not see' but 'you will see that I live'. And then because of me, 'you also will live'. These simple words can offer us a poetry of hope, even within our numbness of these days. He is inviting us to see something that the merely human 'world' cannot see. The life he spoke of lay beyond the darkness of his own death: it is the life that explodes for all of us with his resurrection. So Kathleen has not gone on her journey alone. And we pray to trust, in our darkness, what she now knows in her new light, that Jesus is our Way: because of him she sees and lives; because of him we, too, in our different way, can see and live.

DEATH OF A PARENT

Still with Us

John Lyng OSA

READINGS: ACTS 10:34-36, 42; ROM 5:5-11; MT 5:1-12

In the course of the last thirty years, my mother wrote letters to me which included news of funeral Masses in this church and the burials that followed. And, I suppose, for forty years before that, she wrote similar letters to her sister and brothers in places even farther away. They were the funerals of the fathers and mothers, the brothers and sisters, husbands, wives and even children of most of you here today. Today, her turn has come. Sooner or later, it will be ours. And that, as we say, is the way with life.

When in prayer we remember the dead of any family, we remember the dead of all. And being human, we remember most sharply our own, those of our own house. Uppermost in some of your minds today are, no doubt, relatives of your own who died much younger and much more unexpectedly than our mother. The years are marks on our journey from birth to death. But they are like reversed milestones along the road; they only show us how far we have gone, not how far we have left to go. God decides that. So, some left early and some late. We pray for them all because they are important to us and so we talk of them to our God. It's natural. They have all gone before us and, like ourselves, they are in need of God's mercy.

The ones that went before us left their mark on us; and that is putting it far too mildly. They didn't just mark us: they made us and shaped us and so are with us still. They are with us in the very shape of our bodies, in the way we walk or talk, in the things we enjoy and the things we fear, in the things we're good at and the things we couldn't do well in a fit; they're with us in the way we think, in the very way we blink our eyes, or move our hands, our every tic and mannerism. They are part of ourselves and will always remain so.

We only seem to outlive our fathers and mothers. Even if they have gone ahead of us, they are still with us because they are in us. They refuse to go away. When we have to deal closely with death we are confused; we are upset; the familiar things of life are turned upside down. When we meet people who have lost someone close to them, we are glad to do anything we can to help. And that is good and necessary. But when it comes to what we feel, what we think, or what we should say about a death that is close to us, especially if that death is unexpected, we are uncomfortable or maybe even lost. When a child asks questions about the death of somebody it loves, it's hard to give satisfactory answers. And this is true no matter how strong or well-informed we are. Because death is the great proof of our weakness, the proof that we do not have all the answers, that the last word always lies with God, just as the first word was his too.

Death is a loss, a separation that we cannot avoid and the parting is always sore. It is sometimes said that funerals can be joyful occasions, but I think that's a mistake. As we look to the salvation and eternal life of the one who has died, what mingles with the sadness of the mourning Christian is not joy, but hope. The second reading today tells us that our hope does not deceive us. It is founded on the one who died for us and defeated death for us. That is why Jesus could speak the strange words of today's gospel: 'Blessed are those who mourn.' The sadness of those who mourn is real sadness, but it does not blot out hope and expecta- tion that where they have gone we will follow. We follow them to a place where all that is broken will be mended, all sickness cured, and happiness is found in what is true and good.

The mourning Christian is reminded of the highest joy, the resurrection, the defeat of death. When all hope and expectation for this life has melted away, when there is no longer any human

answer, what awaits us is not the end but our Father. So, while
death is a separation, it is also a homecoming. We believe this
because we believe that Christ was raised from the dead. Paul
says Christ's resurrection is a pledge to us, a guarantee from God,
signed and sealed, that just as he raised Jesus he will raise us into
his presence. The Christian faith does not help us to escape from
death. It does not sweeten the bitterness of death. When we
come to death we are at our very poorest. We come into this
world with nothing. We leave in the same condition. Even if in
the short years between our birth and our death we rule king-
doms and own millions. But Christ was there before us. He was
at his poorest and weakest when he came to death. He was
stripped of all respect and power, stripped even of his clothes.
On the first Good Friday no resurrection was known. Isaiah's
prophesy became a reality in him 'Without beauty, without
majesty we saw him, no looks to attract our eyes ... a man to
make people cover their faces.' Death is so often like that: something to make people cover their faces. We saw with our mother,
and many of you saw with your own, someone who was a pillar
of strength in mind and body become weak and helpless, confused and broken. This is hard to take. But resurrection faith
assures us that, at the final point of human weakness and defeat,
at the moment when we are brought to nothing, we meet God
and are raised by him.

Each of us is a tenant. Anything we have in this life has been
given to us on trust by God. We hold only temporary possession.
We are each given a small part of God's farm or vineyard to culti-
vate. Of course, we don't all get the same quality plot of land.
Some of us get the rich land of good health, good fortune, kind
friends and high abilities, while others get the hard ground of
poverty, misfortune and maybe unjust treatment. But we can be

sure of this: our landlord, God, makes merciful allowance for
these differences when we go to pay the rent.

As we talk and think about men and women who have come

to the end of their strength, we would be poor Christians indeed
if we forget those who do the hard and silent work of taking care
of them. Some names come to my mind and others will come to
yours.

My mother, and all the others we remember today, have gone
round the corner ahead of us, and the manner of their going is
no longer relevant. What does matter is that while here, they, in
their different ways, showed us some of the goodness that God
puts into men and women. It was, largely, through them that
God has been good to us. So, we give thanks to God for their
lives and it is with confidence that we pray to the same God to
give them eternal rest.

DEATH OF A SPOUSE

'Love One Another'

Betty Maher

READING: JN 11:32-36 'Jesus wept'

I have chosen this particular part of John's gospel for this
eucharist today because I find that in these few short verses we
learn that we are not alone; Jesus, too, felt the pain which the
death of a loved one brings; nowhere is the vulnerability, and
therefore the sheer humanity, of Jesus more clearly shown than
in this story. And it is in his humanity that we ourselves learn
what it is to be fully human.

And, as we mourn … today, I try to find some comfort from
knowing that Jesus, too, experienced that very pain which we
know today and, despite the fact that he was the most perfect of
human beings – or perhaps because of it, since he must also have
been the most sensitive – he too, grieved.

And, like so many of us at a time like this, he, I believe, could
not, as we often cannot, find adequate words to comfort those
whose loss is greatest today. At a time when Mary and Martha
most needed comfort, Jesus found himself unable to go to them
straight away, and he must have been acutely conscious of his
inadequacy – the inadequacy of the human condition. He, too,
was grappling with and trying to come to terms with pain and
loss, and at the same time was trying to pluck up the courage to
face the pain of his friends.

It took him several days to arrive at their house. Perhaps he
felt that his own pain would compound theirs, and theirs his.
And yet he knew, I am sure, as we also know, that we need to be
with each other, supporting each other, at such times as this.
Human frailty, however, does not always make this easy.

And so what if we, too, weep, as Jesus wept? Perhaps the important thing is that we are together, even if at this moment we feel quite unable to find 'the right words' to comfort one another. In such situations as today, we have to hold on to the hope and belief that our actions will speak for us, that our presence to one another will demonstrate our love and concern.

I am sure that many here present are lucky, in that they may have a lively faith, and those who have are truly blessed; those who believe can look forward, and find relevance in the rest of this gospel story, and to a time when we will meet our beloved one again. Many can and do hope and trust that the time will come when, as we have been promised, there will be no more tears, no more separations, no more searing pain of loss. And it is on this hope that many of us manage to continue.

But we also know that faith and belief are gifts, and gifts are not won; a gift is just that – something which is given. No doubt there are others here who for some reason cannot believe. And if we know that there are those among us today who are weeping, and who feel they cannot hope or look forward, then perhaps weeping with them is all that we can do; we may simply have to try to stand with them in the great darkness that the question of death brings up, not just for some, but for us all. To try to live through that pain with one another, believers and non-believers alike, may be the only course, as we all face the dark questions which death brings, and to which there are no facile answers.

Maybe, for those who profess to believe, today is a little easier than for those who cannot believe; but then again, maybe not. What should be and what is are not always the same. Perhaps there are also those today who, in spite of strong religious beliefs on 'ordinary' days, find that today, faced with the stark reality of death, there is no light in the distance for them.

Should this be so, then perhaps it may be comforting to remember that this very darkness touched Jesus himself; no doubt the death of Lazarus reminded Jesus, as all deaths remind all of us, that he himself would soon have to face his own dark-ness. Often I think that this is a large part of the pain we feel when someone we love dies. Of course we mourn because we will not see ... alive again in this life, but we also know, even as we try to comfort one another, that this is the one thing we all have in common. Tomorrow, it may be my turn.

So, as we mourn today, for our loved friend ..., for ourselves, and for the others who mourn beside us, let us remember that Jesus, too, mourned, and he, too, wept, both for himself and for those who were close to him. And perhaps we might remember also that maybe the only way Jesus may have of reaching out to those most in pain could be through our loving presence to each other, as we mourn together.

As Christians, this, I think, is what we are asked to do.

DEATH OF A SINGLE PERSON

The Souls of the Virtuous

Aidan Ryan

READINGS: WIS 3:1-6, 9; MT 5:1-12

Those of you who attend funerals frequently will be very familiar with today's first reading. It is probably the most frequently used reading of all at funeral Masses. It could even become so familiar that we no longer hear what it is saying. So today, as we give back into the hands of God the soul of Mary Byrne, I suggest that we look more closely at it.

It is from a part of the Old Testament called the Book of Wisdom. Now, wisdom is a very rich word in the scriptures. It indicates something much deeper than intelligence or cleverness. Wisdom is having a sense of what is really important in life, and what is secondary or less important. It is the ability to discern what is of lasting value and what is of passing concern. It is a capacity to see things in the light of eternity and from God's point of view. Mary Byrne was a person who had something of all this in her approach to life, so it is especially appropriate that we should read from the Book of Wisdom at her funeral. So let me pick just three sentences from the first reading, sentences that throw light on the mystery of death in a general way, and today, for us, suggest ways of looking at the death of Mary Byrne.

The first sentence in the reading says 'the souls of the virtuous are in the hands of God'. Mary was a good living person all her life and now her soul is in God's hands – the loving, welcoming, warm hands of her creator. In what better or safer place could she be?

Then the line 'slight was their affliction, great will their blessings be' – Mary had her share of loneliness and sorrow and her share of pain in her final illness. But all of that is over now, and it pales into insignificance in the blessed happiness and joy of the vision of God in heaven.

Then the last line: 'grace and mercy await those he has chosen'. Many years ago, God chose Mary in baptism to be his beloved child, on whom his favour would always rest. Now he welcomes her with his grace, which is the gift of his free and unconditional love, and his mercy, which is his compassionate understanding of human weakness and sinfulness, and his readiness and eagerness to forgive and to welcome us, just as we are in our imperfections and limitations.

So as we escort Mary by our prayers towards her final destination in heaven, we thank God for his constant presence with her in life and in death. We pray for the wisdom to understand something of what God has prepared for those who love him, or even try to love him. We commend the gentle and virtuous soul of Mary into his loving hands.

DEATH OF A PASTOR

At home in Zion

Terence P. McCaughey

READINGS: PS 130; PHIL 3:4-14; JN 14:1-6, 27
ADDRESS, DRAWN FROM PHIL 3:4-14

I don't really think any of us here today will feel that this is the time (nor am I the person) to deliver a eulogy on the life of Thomas Alexander Byers Smith – or even to run over the highlights of his career. There'll be another time for that, and other places. This is rather the time quite simply to thank God for him; and that is exactly what we are doing.

But perhaps it would help us to focus on that act of thanksgiving, if we were able to think about him now, with more than half an eye on that passage from Paul's Epistle to the Philippians which we read just now. Paul writes:

If anyone else thinks that they have grounds for confidence in the flesh, I have more:
– circumcised on my eighth day;
– of the people of Israel;
– of the tribe of Benjamin;
– a Hebrew of the Hebrews;
– as to righteousness under Law, blameless.

The man we render thanks for today was just such a person: from the very start he had a lot going for him. If anyone had something to boast of, he had more than most. I think it would be true to say that Alec Smyth belonged to a generation of people in our Irish Presbyterian Church who were, by upbringing and training, thoroughly at home in Zion. I don't think this always made them at ease in it. But this church's peculiar way of doing things at any rate held no mysteries for them; they had been familiar with those ways almost since before they could remember. They could, in a way, take it all just as they found it – a little like the way children, as they grow up, come to take their parents for granted – respecting them, of course, but often also smiling at them in a kindly way, sometimes too being a little irritated or even exasperated by the parents' ingrained or seemingly unchanging habits. Actually, quite early on Alec Smyth joined the ranks of those who appreciatively recognised that there are other ways of doing things – some of them as good, or even better than our own. It is also true to say that he lived long enough to be concerned about this church, rather the way that loving parents often are as they have to stand by and watch their children make their own mistakes. *Concerned* he may have been, from time to time, but he did not *tremble* for the Ark, or stretch out a fussy or a nervous hand to steady it.

He had what he *could* have gloried in; but he did *not*. Certainly it would be quite wrong to suggest that he took the gifts God had given him so freely for granted ... gifts of mind or personally, a loving home-life or whatever. I don't think he ever mistook the things that God had done *for* him or *through* him, and imagined that these things were accomplishments of *his*. This man, who had so much going for him, himself knew (and he taught *us*) that everything we ever do that may turn out to be even remotely worthwhile or constructive, is really the work of the Spirit *in* us, 'working to do that which is well-pleasing in God's sight'. By word and example he made it clear that what is happening to us in this world is that the Christ who 'once took hold' of us, is patiently 'perfecting' us – is adapting us (if we will let him) more and more, to make us into appropriately fashioned instruments to his hand.

He would always be the first to say to *us*, as Paul said to the Philippian Christians:

My friends, I do not reckon myself to have got hold of it yet ... I have not reached the point of perfection, but I do press forward, *hoping* ... hoping to take hold of that for which Christ once (long ago) took hold of *me*.

Paul even speaks of 'forgetting what is behind' – and by that strange phrase I think he means *gratefully leaving behind* everything, both the good and the ill, the better to be able to take hold of the gifts God still has in store.

In these last years since his stroke, he could easily *not* have put the past behind; he could have brooded on it, and refused to look forward. His nurses set him new goals and he did try to reach them – and succeeded. Even before that illness, he had lost his dear Nora (just when they might have hoped to have had so much more time together) and that was something he could never forget. But he did not allow his memories to *swamp* him. Instead, he pressed forward ... and even in times of diminished strength there survived from earlier times his sense of fun, his quick eye for the ridiculous and that quiet courtesy.

His family says thanks today for lots of things the rest of us know little of. But scarcely anyone here today does not have cause to be thankful for something God gave us through the life among us of Alec Smyth.

And, next to his family, that applies especially to his congregations. For the parish, the congregation of Christians listening together for God's word and celebrating the sacraments – *that* was *his* chosen sphere of work ... more than committees and boards however important they are in the church's life as a whole. I like to think that, in electing him moderator of its 1959 meeting, the Assembly was affirming that preference of his.

Many of us remember gratefully his leading in prayer; it was never affected or forced. It was very natural and *confident* but it never tipped over into what John Donne called 'being over-fellowly with God'. Certainly not! It never presumed: it never took for granted.

The same was true of his preaching. It was basically direct, simple, straight forward. But it was never facile, and to the end he prepared afresh for each occasion. He was in line with Martin Luther who said once about preaching:

> I do not fear to preach badly. What I *do* tremble at is the prospect of speaking *of* God before God's face.

So now he has taken leave of us, his friends, as one who did experience the power of the resurrection of the crucified one here already in this world, and conveyed something of that power to us. He quits our sight for now, still not *claiming* perfection or complete adequacy, but still moving forward to take hold of that for which Christ once took hold of *him*.

TRAGIC DEATH

Waiting Beyond Words

Niall Ahern

READING: MK 15:33-39 *[handwritten: Mark 15 - 33 - 37]*
[handwritten: The Death of Jesus / Luke 22 - 44 - 46]

Silence is really the only response to death, but when death happens tragically even the silence is inadequate. In the Book of Lamentations we are told that it is good to wait in silence for the Lord to save and that is really all we can do when death strikes tragically. Wait. All we can do is wait.

We have to wait on God because in tragedy God seems absent. What he has allowed happen is so violent; is so corrupt; is so unnatural – that we can only wait to see if he can make any sense of the event which makes no sense to us.

The question is always – Why? Why can a good God allow such terrible sadness to enter into a person's life? The tragedy could have been avoided. There were so many circumstances which could have gone the other way. Why did he let it happen to me – to my family – to my community? We have to wait on words to form any answer.

And here words are always small. Tragedy has no place for small words of comfort, and even the gospel words of God's love and care and tenderness seem a parody of whom he truly is. Like the people in the crowd in Elie Wiesel's book *Night* who cried out as the young boy lay dying on the cross, 'Where is your God now?' – the question always in tragedy is, 'Where is God now?' And the answer comes back to us as it did to them, 'He is here – he is hanging on the tree.'

God is in tragedy. The God we believe in always inhabits our sadness. He always desires to be at the centre of those events in our lives which we cannot understand ourselves. A tragic death,

more than any other event, causes us to live the mystery of faith.
Tragedy proclaims the mystery of faith. Isn't that what we say at
Mass – Christ has died, Christ is risen, Christ will come again.
There is no understanding tragedy except within the mystery of
faith. Such mystery goes beyond words.

Tragic death faces us with the mystery of life itself – not with
circumstances of birth or with length of days or with conditions
of living or even with the moment of dying. The mystery is that
life was given to us at all. And it is the quality of our living, rather
than the detail of our dying, which is of most significance.
William Blake tells us:

'We are put on this earth a small space

that we might learn to bear the beams of love.'

That's the focus to which we are invited today. Not the horror of
death's visitation, but rather the beams of love. The harrowing of
this moment cannot – dare not – obliterate the love which
inhabited this life; a life cut down by a kind of wayward careless-
ness, but a life we celebrate today. And we celebrate silently
because words of love are most poignantly articulated in the
heart and not in the head.

The horror of today somehow invites us to celebrate all that
was loving and lovely and tender and worth cherishing in the
midst of this unexpected and intrusive death. Each one here
knows and experienced something of the love sent out by the one
we mourn, and no act of love sent out into the abyss of time
comes back unclaimed or unheralded.

Let us claim and herald all that was good and noble and pure
in this life, so suddenly physically terminated. We will not be
overcome by the tragedy alone – but rather will be possessed by
the life which was larger than death. This life of love was shared
with us. And may it be so eternally.

And what harm if we stand in embarrassed silence or wait in a
togetherness beyond definition? The disclosure of the mystery of
God requires waiting. To know that we stand together in some

way authentically and real – we must wait beyond words. But God is in the waiting and speaks love in our hearts. The one who has been wrenched from us was God waiting in love for us. The love we knew has returned to the love that made it. Why did this happen now? Why at all? We don't know. But with Thornton Wilder we do know:

> '... we ourselves shall be loved for a while and forgotten. But that love will have been enough. All our impulses of love return to the love that made them. Even memory is not necessary for love. There is a land of the living and a land of the dead and the bridge is love – the only survival, the only meaning.'

TRAGIC DEATH

Suspended in disbelief

John Littleton

READINGS: WIS 3:1-6, 9; PS 114; LK 12:35-40 *[handwritten annotation]*

Tragedy always stuns us. This is especially true when we experience the tragic and sudden death of someone we love dearly. We are shocked as individuals and we are visibly shaken as a community when we learn about the unexpected and premature death of someone we have known so well. We are numbed by the suddenness and the horror of it. We cannot understand it. We have so many questions and we have no answers. We have no satisfactory explanations. We do not want to believe or accept that the person we have known so well and loved so much is dead. In a sense, we are paralysed. We are suspended in disbelief.

Today there is a huge emptiness in our hearts because Margaret, whom we have known and loved, has been taken from us. It is so unfair and so cruel that she has been taken away from us in this way. Margaret was so young and full of life. Her work in this world was not finished. She was in the prime of her life and she was healthy. She still had so much to do and so much to give to other people. We are tempted to say that if she had been elderly – and her death had not been so sudden and tragic – we could accept it. We would be sad, of course, but we could accept her death in such circumstances. It is no wonder, then, that we are devastated at this time. Our grief is enormous. What are we to do? How are we to cope?

Today, we need more than ever to listen attentively to the message of the word of God. Only our faith in God can sustain us and prevent us from remaining suspended in disbelief as we mourn Margaret's death and struggle to cope with our sense of loss. Only the word of God can offer us consolation and hope when we are confronted with the frailty and uncertainty of human life.

Everyone here today can identify so easily with what has been read to us in the first reading from the Book of Wisdom: 'their going looked like a disaster, their leaving us like annihilation.' These words certainly apply to Margaret's untimely death. However, we must also listen to the reassurance, concerning Margaret and many other people who have died, offered to us through the Word of God in the Book of Wisdom: 'but they are in peace ... those who are faithful will live with him in love; for grace and mercy await those he has chosen.' Our faith in the risen Christ encourages us to hope that Margaret is now in peace and enjoying eternal life. We pray that, through God's mercy and forgiveness, Margaret has made her own the words of the response to the psalm: 'I will walk in the presence of the Lord in the land of the living.' Even so, we will continue to pray for her and ask her to pray for us.

But what about us who remain behind? What about us who gather here around Margaret's dead body and, in particular, Margaret's family members who are heartbroken? The word of God, in addition to reassuring us about Margaret, has a relevant and compelling message for us too – a message which, if we listen to it and act accordingly, will ensure that we will be ready for death whenever it comes, whether suddenly in tragic circumstances or slowly at the end of a terminal illness or in old age. In the gospel reading from Luke which was read to us, Jesus says: 'You too must stand ready, because the Son of Man is coming at an hour you do not expect.' Strange words, perhaps, but true words. None of us knows when our life in this world will end. How many of us are ready for death at this moment? The only meaningful way to be ready for death is to prepare purposefully by loving God and all God's people in everything we do.

So there is a definite lesson for us to learn during these sorrowful and lonely days. The lesson is to begin to learn not to be surprised by surprises, or the suddenness of the unexpected. Life and death are mysterious and, therefore, full of surprises. Some of these surprises are remarkably rewarding and happy; others are disturbing in their sadness. We need to prepare for the unexpected. We will never be unprepared if we use properly the various opportunities and possibilities given to us in life. We need to celebrate life and live it fully while we have it. Then, when tragedy happens, indeed we will be shocked and stunned. But we will not remain suspended in disbelief for too long because, even in our grief, our Catholic faith will enable us to continue to live in hope until we meet God in death.

TRAGIC DEATH – BY SUICIDE

'Jesus walks with us in our suffering'

Martin Delaney

READING: LK 24:35-48

[handwritten: EMMAUS JERUSALEM THE APPEARANCE of Xst]

I'm standing here this morning before this great gathering of people brought together by the common bond of the tragic death of a young person we all knew. I am very much aware that all words are inadequate to temper our grief or to begin to heal the pain being so keenly felt in this church this morning. And yet we have to talk, as we have been talking over the last few days. Since John died we have all been telling stories, asking questions and getting no answers. We all want to know why this had to happen. Was there something we could have done? Why? Why? Why? For so many people in this church today, the death of John last Thursday has turned their world upside down. We have all been plunged into a great darkness and we are desperately looking for a little light.

I presume that no one here this morning is unaware that John took his own life. I believe it is important that we acknowledge it publicly, to hear those words spoken aloud and not just whisper them privately among ourselves. In this way we can try to deal with it. We can perhaps begin to acknowledge that, in addition to the terrible loss and grief that comes with the sudden and tragic death of someone so young, there may also be feelings of anger within our hearts. Anger with John, anger with society, anger with ourselves. We will probably never know why this tragedy happened but what we do know is that John was greatly loved by many people, particularly by his parents, Maureen and Jimmy, and by his brothers and sisters. John also loved them and a great many other people too, and somehow in his troubled heart John believed that what he was doing was out of love for those in his life. This is very difficult for us to understand but it may be some consolation to know that just as John had brought so much love to others in life, he also believed that his death was a loving act too, that somehow he was lifting a burden from your shoulders.

But for you, Maureen and Jimmy, and for all of you who loved John so much, I know that this death has brought you a great burden of sorrow and pain. I would like to share something with you which I hope will make some sense to you. Every year I visit many primary schools around the diocese and I am always amazed by the variety of questions about religion which the children have. However, there is one question which I am asked more than any other: Why is Good Friday called *Good?* How could the cruelty of the crucifixion ever be seen as good? In asking this question, the children are focusing in one of the ageless mysteries of our Christian faith. Why did Jesus have to suffer on Calvary? Why could he not have climbed down from the cross triumphantly when surely the Roman soldiers and the Centurion would have dropped to their knees in homage, and the people of Jerusalem, who only a few short hours earlier had demanded his death, would have poured up the hill to worship him? The whole world would soon have known that certainly Jesus Christ was the Son of God.

But this did not happen. It did not happen because, as Jesus told the two disciples on the road to Emmaus and again reminds the frightened gathering in the upper room of today's gospel: It was necessary that the Christ should suffer these things. The scriptures for centuries had been foretelling this very truth. Necessary, not by some abstract truth or law of nature, but because this was the way God wanted it. This was the way God wanted it, and Jesus in free obedience accepted this charge from his Father. But it was precisely through this emptying of himself, through his acceptance of suffering and death, that he won victory over death.

But why? Why a blood-soaked death when surely there were other ways open to an all powerful, all knowing God? Why a death so horrific that Jesus himself asked to be spared of it at the eleventh hour? The honest answer is that we really do not know. We get some clue from Jesus himself when he talks of his suffering and death as being rooted in God's love for each of us: 'Greater love than this no man has, than he lay down his life for his friends.' (Jn 15:13) Somehow, by rising from the dead and conquering suffering and pain, after he had fully entered into the darkness and despair which that very suffering and pain brought him, Jesus could powerfully identify and empathise with our struggle and pain. And not only could he identify with our suffering and pain, but he could show us a way through it, give it a purpose.

If Jesus had triumphantly climbed down from the cross and escaped all the human suffering that went with it, would he have anything to say to John's heartbroken family and friends today? I think not. As it is, the only real source of hope and healing for this gathering this morning is that somehow our suffering and pain today is intimately linked with the suffering and death of Jesus Christ, the Son of God. But just as our suffering and pain, and John's suffering and pain and death, are linked with Jesus, so too the resurrection of Jesus allows us all the exact same hope. 'So you see how it was written that the Christ would suffer and on the third day rise from the dead.' (Lk 24:47)

Note: In cases of a tragic death like this, the preacher should discuss the content of the homily with the bereaved family beforehand.

TRAGIC DEATH – BY SUICIDE

De Profundis

John Wall

READINGS: EZEK 34:11-12; 15-16; PS 129; ROM 8:14-18; JN 11:17-27

'If only'... words we often use, but especially when we experience tragedy or great stress – like the sadness all of us experienced at the shock news of this tragic passing of Stephen. And we find exactly the same sentiment expressed by Mary in the gospel today. She says to Jesus *if only* you were here' this would not have happened. It's a natural reaction.

I remember when I was a student in the seminary, a very wise and experienced teacher on the staff told us: 'When you meet a situation of extreme frustration, as all tragedies are, you will find two strong emotions – blame and guilt. Both are natural but neither is helpful. They are just expressions of the anger of frustration.'

The frustration is felt because Stephen was much loved – loved by his parents, family and many friends. If care could have kept him, he would still be with us.

Stephen was a fine young man, enthusiastic in his generosity. He was also a very sensitive person, perhaps too sensitive for his own good. In his sensitivity he felt things deeply. And that same sensitivity that gave him a sympathy and a thoughtfulness for others, caused him to feel the pain of life more keenly than others might feel it.

Drugs were taken initially as an anaesthetic against the pain of life and because they were readily available – and then continued because of the entrapment of addiction that he so bravely tried to overcome. And we know that it was his frustration with that addiction that led to the tragedy of his death.

We leave all judgement to God, with whom 'there is mercy

and fullness of redemption'. In the funeral prayers we pray that he will 'forgive any sin we committed through the frailty of our human nature'. We also recall that 'God remembers the good that we have done and forgives our sins'. In that Spirit we pray today for Stephen, remembering the words of Jesus from the cross: 'Father, forgive them, for they know not what they do.'

And we pray too that those who loved Stephen dearly will be able to forgive and let go of any anger they may feel from the frustration of his passing.

In our second reading, St Paul is prompted by the Spirit to cry out: 'Abba, Father' in prayer to God – surely the God of Ezekiel in our first reading, who will search for his sheep 'and will rescue them from all places where they have been scattered, on a day of clouds and thick darkness'. Surely, he will bring Stephen safely home.

We cry out too to the Christ of our gospel today, the Christ of our frustrations. The Christ who was approached by Mary in *her* frustration at the death of her brother. The Christ who wept for his friend, Lazarus.

We know, as Mary did, that all *will* be well, that Jesus is the resurrection and the life. But what do we do in the meantime? There are a lot of people out there, hurting and in need of our help. There is a lot to be done in the battle against drugs. We pray for that gift, to work out our frustrations by practical caring and following the example of Jesus in the gospel. In that way Stephen's death will not be in vain, but rather it can become an occasion to spur us on to look after those who really need us.

DEATH AFTER A LONG ILLNESS

Life is changed, not ended

John Littleton

READING: MK 15:33-39 *THE DEATH of Jesus*

Today is a sad and lonely day. At last, Michael, a husband, a father, a neighbour and a friend to many people, has died. He has gone from this life. But, in a sense, today is also a day of relief, particularly for his wife and children who sat at his bedside and watched him dying slowly and, until the last few days, painfully. Now he suffers no more pain. He is no longer distressed. He no longer struggles to die. He is finally in peace and we are grateful for this.

Sometimes it seems that God has deserted us. When most people, including Michael, discover that they are terminally ill, they are usually frightened and they plead with God, asking him to restore them to health. They may become angry with God when, having asked for his help, he seems to do nothing; at least, God does not respond in the way they would wish. This is especially true regarding the pain and the distress associated with serious and terminal illness. Their faith in God's goodness and care is challenged and tested. Like Jesus dying on the cross, they may cry: 'My God, my God, why have you deserted me?'

Then there are family members, neighbours and friends, who watch helplessly and in anguish as someone they love gradually wastes away and dies. We pray that God will intervene in some miraculous manner and make him better. We may even begin to bargain with God in the vain hope that our bargaining will make a difference. But, in the end, the person we love dies and there is nothing we can do about it. Again, like Jesus dying on the cross, we may also cry: 'My God, my God, why have you deserted me?'

Today, as we gather in church at Michael's funeral, in the midst of our grief and sadness we are professing our Christian faith in the resurrection of the dead and eternal life. We are affirming our belief – although it does not always seem reasonable – that, while all life on this earth is terminal and while death is a fact of life, death is not the end for Michael or, indeed, for any of us. There is life after death: life that never ends. Even in our sadness, we believe that Michael's death in this life has been his birth into eternal life. Michael lived to die and, ironically, he died to live. This is the real mystery of life and death. Therefore Michael's life is changed, not ended. It is our prayer that Michael is now enjoying eternal life with God.

Michael experienced much suffering towards the end of his earthly life. But, in our hearts, we know that suffering can have great value – no matter how incomprehensible this may seem to us today. Through pain and suffering we learn what it means to embrace the cross of Christ. Like Jesus, dying on the cross, our faith is tested when we experience suffering, and when we witness suffering in other people's lives. However, just as God did not desert Jesus, he does not desert us. And he did not desert Michael. It is our hope that Michael's suffering in this life has not been in vain but, instead, has prepared him to live a life that has changed, not ended, and rest in God's peace and love forever.

LK 23:44-46. "(WAS NOW ABOUT NOON, AND DARKNESS CAME OVER THE WHOLE LAND UNTIL THREE IN THE AFTERNOON WHILE THE SUN'S LIGHT FAILED; AND THE CURTAIN OF OF THE TEMPLE WAS TORN IN TWO THEN JESUS CRIED WITH A LOUD VOICE, SAID 'FATHER, INTO YOUR HANDS I COMMEND MY SPIRIT.' HAVING SAID THIS, HE BREATHED HIS LAST.'

Gratitude in Grief

Ambrose Tinsley OSB

READING: LK 23:44-46

(The following homily was given, not with the funeral Mass, but on the previous evening when the body had been taken to the church.)

This passage which we have just heard continues by recording the reaction of the soldier who was standing by the cross. He praised God, we are told, proclaiming that the one who died was certainly a person who was good and great. Tonight, as we now pay our last respects to Joan, I feel that that same kind of tribute should be paid to her as well. That may sound almost trite, like some of those remarks which people make without reflection when a person whom they knew has died. But, even if it does, that doesn't mean that it cannot be true. The Joan whom I knew in her final years was certainly both good and great, and I do not have any doubt at all that her considerate and gentle presence will be sorely missed.

Our sympathies, of course, go in a special way to John her husband, to Helena and Siobhán, to Joan's own parents who were able to come down to see her some few days ago. Indeed our sympathies to all who have been shocked by what may have appeared to some to have been quite a sudden, unexpected death.

But Joan had no illusions. After her mastectomy, she had prayed for the gift of three more years. And God was good. He granted her request. She then not only did all that she could for her own family, but started visiting the patients in a nearby hospice too. In that way she repeatedly and with courage faced the dark reality of that disease which also threatened her. The next stage in her journey, which I have been able to identify, took place last summer when she was at home. There, in the sunshine of her garden, she experienced within herself a feeling that the end for her was not too far away. It was a premonition which, just two months later, turned to physical concern.

One reason why I chose this section of the passion story for the gospel of tonight is that it manifests for us the mind of Christ when he was faced with his approaching death. 'Into your hands I commend my spirit,' he exclaimed. Joan never used those words, at least to me, but her acceptance of what was to happen was complete. Indeed, it seemed at times so total that I felt within myself a certain sense of awe. There seemed to be in her a secret and a sacred depth which gave her strength to face and to accept what was to come. And when it did, she very quietly gave her own spirit to the One in whom she had put all her trust.

The other reason why I chose this gospel passage is because of that short phrase: 'The veil of the temple was torn in two.' Its implication seems to be that people then began to see what had been veiled from them before. For instance, through the death of Christ they recognised in him a goodness which they realised had come from God and, as they later contemplated it, their lives were obviously changed. Indeed, as we have heard, the soldier at the cross perceived a goodness in the one who died and found that, consequently, he was able to give praise to him from whom all goodness comes. Is it too soon for us to do the same? Is it too soon to give God thanks and praise for all the goodness that he has revealed to us through Joan? I know we grieve, how could we not, but I at least find consolation in the words of Jerome, that great human saint who, writing to a friend whose mother had just died, declared, 'we thank God that we had her for so long'. If our own mood today is one of grieving at the loss of someone whom we loved, there surely is a level in our hearts where we are grateful to have known her and to have experienced her goodness in our lives.

It is a pity that this note of gratitude is not expressed explicitly in the funeral rite itself. However, when we gather here tomorrow morning it will be to celebrate the eucharist which is, as its name implies, a service of thanksgiving. Then, despite our grief, we will be asked to give thanks to the Lord our God for all the many blessings which we have received and, consequently, for the ones which came to us through Joan. Perhaps, at such a moment, we will even be aware that she is somehow with us still. If not, that day will surely come and then our gratitude for all that she has done for us, and can do still, will consequently grow.

DEATH OF AN AUTISTIC YOUTH

Genius and Handicap

Eltin Griffin O Carm

READING: LK 10:21-23

They say that the presence of a genius in the home can have as
great an effect on the equilibrium of a family as that of a handicapped child. But when genius and handicapped are combined
in the one child, the challenge seems insuperable. And yet none
of us would have been without Paul. His Adonis-like face and
figure, his utterly beautiful countenance, his enormous height,
his prodigious strength, his intellectual grasp of disparate and
disconnected areas of knowledge – these are aspects of Paul we
will always remember, recall, recount and retell. There were
times when he made incredible demands on his family, on his
parents, on his brothers and sisters, on relations and friends,
times when he upset the entire household, when he threw it into
disorder and confusion – but through his bizarre, strange and
amusing ways he made a distinct and distinctive contribution to
the life of the family, brought out in each and all of them
undreamt of depths of strength, dedication and love. Paul was
the glue in his family even when he became too much for them
to handle any longer and had to be put into special care. He left a
void behind him, a place in the household that could never be
filled.

Paul, in normal circumstances, would have been an undoubted
genius, in the area maybe of higher mathematics or of music. He
might have excelled his parents in artistic expression. Why
should such expression have been denied him? Is it fair that such
genius should be trammelled, should be prevented from expressing itself, leading to extraordinary tantrums and frustration?

I can't claim to have all the answers. I cannot act the part of God except to say that in life we are all trammelled – we are all hindered – we are all prevented through circumstances from giving total expression to all our gifts, no matter how comfortably we may try to arrange our lives. We suffer from the limitations of time and space, from the limitations imposed on us by lack of finance, lack of time, lack of understanding by other people, even those who are close to us, lack of support when it is needed. Our efforts never reach the total degree of perfection we might desire. Limitation is part of life. Many an artist, on seeing or hearing the end product, has been forced to say 'That is not what I meant at all', even though others may hail it as a masterpiece.

It is only in another life that we can let go of limitation, as we enter into a transcendental relationship with the universe, with the whole of creation, with the Heavenly City and with the Master and Lord of the universe, who draws us all into total communion with all that exists and to the transformation of our beings.

For Paul, limitation has given way to limitless possession, to that fulfilment for which his whole being cried out. And so, at the request of Frances, we give thanks to God, as we have done in the gospel this morning, in the words of Mary in the Magnificat.

People will say it is a merciful release. Easy to say, but there is still the pain of letting go. Life is full of letting go. Parents are forever letting go. It is in the numerous letting goes that parents attain their full maturity. They are no longer needed, the prelude may be for the final letting go.

Books, plays and novels have been written on this familiar theme. C. Day Lewis says, in his attractive poem on the subject, 'Love is proved in the letting go.'

34. Come you that are blessed by my Father, inherit the kingdom prepared for you from the foundation of the world; 35 for I was hungry and you gave me food, I was thirsty and you gave me something to drink; I was a stranger and you welcomed me 36 I was naked and you gave me clothing, I was sick and you took care of me; I was in prison and you visited me.

DEATH OF AN UNBELIEVER

Michael Paul Gallagher SJ

READING: MT 25:31-40

We may know that parable of the Last Judgement too well, and so we miss its shock effect. If I try to translate it into more modern language, it is saying, surprisingly, that faith is not on the final examination paper. But love is. Indeed, it is the only topic being examined, because it is God's way of measuring our lives. As St John of the Cross put it, with a certain play of words, 'in the evening of life we will be judged by love'. By the love we lived. And by the Love, capital L, who is God. That parable, then, contains a happy surprise for those who are not sure of God. They are like those people in the judgement story who ask: 'but where did we ever know you?' 'As often as you did it to one of these least of mine, you did so to me.'

Many of you here this morning will realise why this gospel is so fitting for the funeral of our friend Eamon. He was not a church-goer and, indeed, some years ago I remember his talking to me about what he called his 'block about God'. He didn't like the labels 'atheist' or 'non-believer'. Indeed he liked to joke that he believed too much. He believed people, especially if they told him they needed his help in some way – from beggars on the street to those in drug rehabilitation to whom he devoted most of his working life. He believed in his work as making a difference, even when it was tough going or when failures left him angry or hurt.

Perhaps because Eamon encountered so much pain in people, he found it all the harder to believe in God. Is that not true of all of us when we run into the desolations of life? But which God becomes incredible in those darker times? Possibly the God who seems beyond all struggle, the God who is meant to control everything and lets so much tragedy happen. We heard one surprise in the gospel – that love is the measure, that faith is, in a strange sense, secondary.

There is another surprise imaged in front of us above the altar, an image we become so used to seeing that it too loses its shock. On the cross we see a man dying, and we dare to believe that he is dying because of love, because of love for us, and that he is also God among us. The crucifix puts an end to all those pagan images of a God beyond struggle or pain. I wonder, or at least I dare to wonder, whether Eamon ever really had the chance to ponder who this God is, this Crucified One who loved, and suffered because he loved. In prayer for Eamon this morning, we ask that his loving and his suffering carry him to the surprise of Christ's gratitude: 'whenever you cared for all those wounded ones that came your way, you were meeting me.'

A final reflection, more for us who live on than for Eamon who has left this place of searching. If love is the measure, then what difference does faith make? Eamon loved stories. I answer with a story to explore this question about 'why faith, if love is the key?' Once upon a time, there was a queen who asked one of her close friends to carry a bag for her from one village to another. The bag was heavy but the friend carried it because he was asked to do so and because the queen was his friend. When he came back, the queen asked him, 'What did you think was in that bag?' 'I wondered about it but have no idea,' he answered. 'Suppose it was rubbish in the bag,' said the queen, 'would that upset you?' 'It might,' replied the friend, 'but not all that much: I was carrying it because you asked me to.' 'Yes, you carried it without knowing,' said the queen, 'but if you had known there was pure gold in the bag, it would have made a difference.'

We are asked to carry life with love. We are also invited to know the pure gold of faith. Eamon carried much and if he sometimes imagined the gold, perhaps he thought that was too good to be true. On the other side of death he now knows in a way that we cannot, but we can pray that Eamon enjoy that surprising welcome of Christ.

THE CONTRIBUTORS

Niall Ahern is Administrator of St Mary's Cathedral, Sligo.

Martin Delaney, parish of St John, Kilkenny, is Diocesan Adviser for Religious Education in the diocese of Ossory.

Desmond Forristal, writer and dramatist, is Parish Priest of Dalkey, Co Dublin.

Michael Paul Gallagher SJ is a writer and teacher.

Eltin Griffin O Carm is a liturgist, writer and preacher.

Benedict Hegarty OP is a scripture scholar and Prior of St Saviour's, Dublin.

Dermot A. Lane, theologian and writer, is Parish Priest of Balally, Dublin.

John Littleton is a theologian and curate in the parish of Doon, Co Limerick.

Dick Lyng OSA is Parish Priest of St Augustine's, Galway.

John Lyng OSA is an Augustinian missionary in Maiduguri, Nigeria.

Terence P. McCaughey is a theologian and minister of the Presbyterian Church in Ireland.

Brendan McConvery CSsR is a scripture scholar and preacher.

Brian McKay O Carm is a formation director and retreat guide.

Betty Maher is a writer whose latest book is *Called to be a Nuisance: Reflections from the Fringe.*

Aidan Ryan is Parish Priest of Carrickedmond, Co Longford.

Richard Sheehy is a chaplain at Trinity College, Dublin.

Ambrose Tinsley OSB is a monk of Glenstal Abbey.

John Wall is Parish Priest of Seville Place Parish, Dublin.

Thomas R. Whelan CSSp, liturgist, is Director of Studies at the Kimmage Mission Institute, Dublin.